THE DECISION
Gaining Immediate Control Of Your Life

Mecheline Muhammad

JAKC PUBLISHING
RALEIGH, NORTH CAROLINA

Copyright © 2019 by Mecheline Muhammad

All rights reserved. No part of this book may be used or reproduced in any manner whatsoever without written permission from the publisher except in the case of brief quotations embodied in critical articles and reviews. For additional information, please contact jakcpubllc@gmail.com

Disclaimer: This book is intended to be motivational and to promote personal growth. The Content is not intended to be a substitute for professional medical advice, diagnosis, or treatment. Always seek the advice of your physician or other qualified healthcare provider with any questions you may have regarding a medical or mental health condition. In the event you wish to apply ideas contained herein, you are taking full responsibility for your actions. Neither the publisher nor the copyright holder(s) may be held liable for any misuse or misinterpretation of the information in this publication.

The Decision / Mecheline Muhammad - First Edition: 2019

ISBN 978-1-7337206-0-1 (Hardcover)
ISBN 978-1-7337206-1-8 (Paperback)
ISBN 978-1-7337206-2-5 (eBook)
ISBN 978-1-7337206-3-2 (Workbook)

Mecheline Muhammad / JAKC PUBLISHING
P.O.BOX 1038
Greenville NC 27835
www.jakcpublishing.com
www.iammechelinemuhammad.com

Book Layout ©2017 BookDesignTemplates.com
Cover Design: Debonair Design Graphics

Ordering Information:

Special discounts are available on quantity purchases by corporations, associations, educators, and others. For details, contact the publisher at the above listed address.

U.S. trade bookstores and wholesalers: Please contact JAKC Publishing by email at jakcpubllc@gmail.com

Contents

Unconscious Behavior 21

The Purge, The Mourning & The Yellow Brick Road 27

    The Purge 28

    The Mourning 29

    The Yellow Brick Road 30

Acceptance & Responsibility 33

Execution: How to Execute with Immediate Results by Taking Action in the Moment 37

    The Giraffe and the Turtle 38

When You're Tired of Mastering Mediocrity 45

Going Before the Judges 51

Holding On While Letting Go -The Law of Detachment 57

The Power of Power 63

    Food For Thought: Awakening Your Power 68

    Tapping Into Your Greatness: Wielding Your Power 69

The Art of Creative Talk-Speak: Being Mindful of How You Talk 73

Change & Adaptability: Are You Adaptable? 79

The Path Less Traveled 87

Desiring From a Beggars Point of View 97

It's in the Little Things 105

Mapping Out the Master Plan 111
Worthiness, Forgiveness, Acceptance & Accountability 117
    Worthiness 118
    Forgiveness 119
    Acceptance & Accountability 122
The Perception of Time 125
Trust, Faith, Hope & Believing 133
Epilogue 139
Bibliography 143

To my husband and children who have supported me throughout my journey, I dedicate this book to you. You have endured, right along with me, the ups and downs from the very beginning of this journey, and for that, I am so very thankful. This journey has been made easier because I've had you all with me along the way. I love you all so very much, and I am ever so grateful, that during my time spent on this earth, I have been blessed to be able to spend it with you.

Abdullah, Quisuana, Oksana, Tahani, Nayala, Jeremiah and Josiah

Acknowledgements

Many people played a part in my becoming the woman that I am today, and I'm grateful to every one of them for every part played. Most especially, the multitude of women, the elders, who've played a role in molding me into this woman that I've become. This thank you is dedicated to YOU! Often times, we don't know the actual effect that we have on people's lives.

We know the saying, a reason, a season or a lifetime. Who's ever to know what part each person who enters into our lives will play, but we enjoy each and every moment given to us to share. I want to take a moment to acknowledge some of the women who've played a significant role in my life. I'm sure that some of them will be surprised to find that they've made such an impact on me.

In no particular order, I'd like to thank:

Sharina Shaw – One little conversation. Not much to it. Just two ladies from elementary school, catching up with each other and speaking casually. You made a comment. A simple phrase that caused me to give serious thought to writing books. Not just one book, but many. You placed a permanent pathway into my train of thought. It has taken years to bring it to fruition, but look at where you're reading this now. ~ Smile

Velecia Williams - You've had many conversations with me where I know you were speaking to me because you felt led to do so. You may not realize this, but you cleared a blockage for me during my last visit to your home. In the midst of all of the love that you shared and imparted my way, you made a statement that helped me to take things for what they are. I won't say too much here since I've written about it in the book, but I'm ever grateful for that moment because it was as if those words were the very reason why I was to come and spend time with you and Kathy at your home on that evening. Sometimes it's just the little things.

Ms. Sheila Harfield – What a lady! Your spirit spreads light! Thank you and Mr. Harfield for taking my husband and me under your wings and giving us an excellent example of what marriage should and could be. Every time we turned around, you were dropping nuggets our way. I want you to know that I heard you. You've been nothing but love and light to and for us since we first met you. I am so grateful to have you in my life.

Dr. Brenda Stephenson – My other, other mother. Lol! From the day I first met you, as if you've known me for years, you've supported me and loved me for who and where I was in any given moment of the time that you've known me. You've been supportive of me, my works, and my business. You've been there from the beginning, unrelenting and always with motherly love. Almost sometimes, as if I'd come from your womb. At least that's how I felt about it. I want you to know that I love you! I wouldn't trade you for the world. You've been an ear when I needed it, guidance when that's what I needed and a stern talking to when it was necessary. Thank you for being who you are in my life.

Ms. Regina Hardy - I've had what I believe to be an angel in my life before. That experience has allowed me to recognize that you were placed exactly where you needed to be, just for me. No one can tell me any different. I know it may look as though I popped into your life, but I can tell you this, all of the years you spent where you were, played its part in how you were able to be the angel in that moment point of our lives. I am ever so grateful to you for stepping into that role so seamlessly and gently leading me towards the path that I was to travel.

Louise Omotto Kessel - You came into my life 18 years ago, and we've shared different sets of moment points throughout the years. No matter how brief some of those moments were, I've always felt your genuine love and caring nature. You introduced me to a way of life that I would come to love in my later years. You've been there for me at critical moments in my life, to which I am so grateful to you. It matters not how much "time" passes between contacts. It always warms my heart to hear from and speak with you. I don't take for granted, not for one moment, the connection that we have.

Tammy Atchison - I've known you, but for a brief moment and I can tell you that the small moment point where we connected was inspiring. People play roles in the lives of others that they're not always aware of. You helped me to stand firm in embracing who and what I was innately born to be. Sometimes it's the little things that we think nothing of. Furthermore, you saw something there, in me, that I could not yet see, that forced me to view myself from a different perspective. I've always been thankful to you for this.

April Brook Lynn Dorcent - My stealth mode operator, writing coach and inspiration. Do you remember when I told you that I'd been playing around with writing a book and that I was going to get to it one day and you stopped me in my tracks and told me . . . "Don't wait?" You seeded the sense of urgency in me that caused me to want to complete a writing project. I've started on many books before The Decision, and I intend to continue working on and finishing them one by one. However, working with you to get started and on the right writing path, has been a highlight for me in this whole experience. You laid it out for me, no holds barred; and forced me, to continuously seek out the very best in my work. Even during the times when I thought I was sending you some of my best written thus far, you still pushed me towards excellence. For a first work, I'm pretty proud of the outcome, and I have you to thank for that. You are a walking example of what I deem to be a successful teacher who leads and teaches by example!

Robin Irvin - What can I say? You are one of the sweetest and gentlest persons that I know. So much so that you make me want to bring out the "gentle" in me. This book is for you just as much as it was for me. Thank you for taking the time to be my proofreader when I needed one. A listening ear when I needed it and a shoulder to lean on when it was needed. I'm proud to call you my friend.

Susan Heath Eaker - The woman who I love to term, my guardian angel. You have, without a doubt, changed the course of my life; at a young and tender age at that. It's as if you were placed in my life to be there at a time when I was to need you the most. Without your guidance, during those tender years, the course of my life would most assuredly have been on a different path, and because of that, I am ever grateful to you and for you. You will always hold a special place in my heart. You are still a guardian angel to me and will always be.

Reverend Claudette Delpino - Your very presence is enough to drop nuggets and instill knowledge without ever having to utter a word; which made your words of wisdom like icing on the cake. You glow with wisdom and intelligence. You never judged and I've always loved that about you. You always spoke, from a "let's get the lesson" point of view. At least that's always been my perspective, and it has helped me to begin approaching my circumstances and situations in this way. For this, I am ever grateful.

There are many others who've come and gone, in and out of my life. All of whom have played one role or another, but all of them beneficial because of the lessons that came with our moments together. Most of them know who they are. I'm thankful to each and every one of you.

Foreword

It is important to note that if you are in a place, mentally and emotionally, that causes you to have thoughts that may lead to your self-inflicted demise, and you are without support and are unable to bring your mindset to a place of peace, PLEASE by all accounts SEEK PROFESSIONAL HELP! You are not expected to have to go through this alone. It was a personal choice for me not to seek professional help and, while I'm glad to say that I made it through without the loss of my life, I know that realistically, that outcome isn't the same for everyone.

Once I'd made my decision (which you'll come to understand better in the coming pages), I considered, but chose not to seek professional help because I believed myself to be capable of handling the situation and bringing myself out of the funk that I was in. Having had the experience of going through deep depression in my early 20's, I'd already experienced working with a professional. I was able to recognize the downward path of which I was spiraling into and I had no desire to go there again. Seeing a professional, worked for me then and, gave me what I needed at the time. You see, my mindset wasn't what it is today. I didn't know half of what I know now, and I needed guidance not from a professional, but an elder.

Still, it took so long to come out of that depression. It was as if I had no control over myself. I remember the feeling of wanting to finally be free of being in that state of deep depression and going back to living a normal life again, but for some reason, I couldn't snap myself back. I knew then, that if I made it out of that bout of depression, I NEVER wanted to sink that deep again. It was like being in quicksand. Even when I thought I was pulling myself out, I was still sinking, slowly but surely.

So by having experienced being deeply depressed before and surviving it; knowing myself for who I am and what I know and believe today, I believed myself to be fully capable of rising above what I was dealing with at that time. So again, if you're at a crossroads, and you're contemplating anything other than a pro-life solution, please seek professional help.

You should know that YOU have something to offer in this life. Your life has a purpose even if it is yet to be discovered. You are worthy of the opportunity to live this life to its fullest, which is whatever YOU deem it to be. At any given time, even when it doesn't appear to be so, YOU ARE IN CONTROL of every aspect of your life. Circumstances and situations will come and go, but how you choose to handle it is where only YOU have control! You determine the outcome because YOU decide how it will affect you and how you will react.

I charge you to take everything that has happened to and for you in this life and use it all, in the now, to build yourself up. All of the good and all of the bad that has happened in your life has been for a reason because nothing is without its purpose in this life. No matter how things may seem or appear to you or others around you, you indeed are in control of your life. Sometimes, it's merely about understanding or the lack thereof and perception. In regards to the others in and around your life, let's get this straight; their opinions, thoughts, and beliefs about YOUR life, is NONE OF YOUR BUSINESS! The sooner you realize, accept and live accordingly to this understanding, your life is already that much better!

It is my desire that this book reaches everyone who is seeking the contents offered within. I consider it a privilege that my works fell into your hands and that you are choosing to read my book. You see while I may not know every individual who will read this book, I am honored that you chose my work and deemed it worthy of reading and giving it a try. I hope that in reading it, that it helps you in whatever way you were hoping for.

Mecheline Muhammad
January 2019

Preface

Congratulations on your first step of working towards elevating to living in your greatness! You have made the first decision of many towards your new beginning. This is a wonderful reason to celebrate because I know, first hand, that even with the best of intentions it's not so easy to get started for some of us. The fact though, that you have this book in your hand and you're reading this page, at this moment, means that it's finally your time!

There are NO mistakes, only lessons! Coincidence is non-existent because everything happens for a reason. I'm a firm believer in this not only because of my convictions, but because the proof has convicted me through experience, that it is true.

No matter how this book came to be in your hands; whether you purchased it, it was gifted, you borrowed it from the library, or it found you, you were meant to be reading this book at this point in your life.

By deciding to read this book, you have started the journey to living as the beautiful, magnificent human being that you are! No more indecisiveness. No more second guessing yourself. No more shying away from living the life that you KNOW you should be living. No more excuses! No more laziness and procrastination. You will no more, live vicariously through the lives of others! Be the person you've always wanted to be. Live the life you've always wanted to live. Speak the words you've always wanted to speak. Do the things you've always wanted to do!

From this point forward living a mediocre life is unacceptable! You are not here to live this life as a drone! You are here for a purpose! You are now and have always been a seeker. Every thought of curiosity that has ever run through your mind at any given point in your life confirms this. We are inherently built to be seekers because seeking inevitably leads us to our purpose and mission in this life and we all come with a purpose and a mission for this life.

From the moment we entered this world, we came directly into the setting that would prepare us for the moment in time when we would be activated to live out our life's purpose. The family you were born into; life's circumstances and the situations that you've had to live through, in and endure, all were for this reason. No matter what walk of life you've come from or are currently living in; you were going to come to this point. I DON'T CARE WHERE YOU ARE IN LIFE, your whole world can and will change with one simple step. You must make THE DECISION.

Introduction: How It All Began
The End That Sparked The Beginning

Hit from every corner of the box that I'd built a world for myself in, my rock bottom didn't creep up on me; it hit me with a bang. We lost our home and was one paycheck away from living on the streets. My business was suffering on the brink of loss until finally, it folded within itself. My children and I were separated from each other; some by choice and others by circumstance and to top it off, my husband decided that in the midst of all of this, it was a good time to try and leave me for another woman.

While my family and I have been dealing with the details of all of the above; as the executor of my household, the owner and operator of my business, the mother of my children and the wife to my husband, the devastation of everything falling apart at once, hit me hard from every corner of my life that I deemed to be the most important to me.

I cried this year for the first time in about ten years. I cried so hard that I could feel all of the years of suppressed emotions, previously unexpressed, just seeping out of me during my weeping. Uncontrollably I sobbed for days on end. In the hotel room of which we were living in, on the road while I was driving (reckless and dangerous I might add), over the phone when I attempted to talk to someone and with the one person with whom I chose to share everything in order to get the hefty load lifted off of my chest.

I had hit a level in my life that was lower than I'd ever been before. I've lived a tumultuous life, and I've experienced my fair share of setbacks, trials, and tribulations throughout my life, but this right here was an all-time low even for me. The lowest I'd ever been and the lowest I cared to go.

I'd found myself contemplating and giving real thought and preparation for taking myself out. From my point of view, at 43, what more could I possibly do? Where could I possibly go after all of this? How could I start over at this age and this point in my life? I had nothing as far as I could see at that time and I was only holding my children back by trying to hold on to them;

fighting the inevitable change taking place that I was so bent on resisting, even if I wasn't consciously trying to resist.

The night came that I was to complete the deed. Get it over and done with and I felt and followed the notion of writing a note to my family; explaining things from my point of view and how it would be better and more beneficial for them once I was no longer a hindrance to them. I'd failed myself, my children, my grandchildren, and even my husband. I dropped the ball somewhere along the way, and this seemed to be the only way to set things right.

Then, to ensure that I'd gotten everything out in the letter, I read it over; and as I was doing so, a switch clicked in me when I heard an inner voice say to me in a far off, authoritative whisper, that I was giving up on myself. What I was getting ready to do wasn't about or for the benefit of my family. It was all about me. Whether or not I was being selfish or merely wallowing in my sorrows, the irreversible action that I was about to take, would only serve to do the opposite of what I wanted it to do for my family.

Then and there I was at a crossroad and needed to make a choice and take immediate action. Whatever direction I went in, I'd have to execute right at that moment. Otherwise, I'd leave room to change my mind. The fact is, at the moment that I stopped and followed the notion of writing a letter to my family, I'd already made my decision. Making a ceremony out of having to decide on what to do was just a formality for the sake of my ego. Either way, that decision sparked a series of other events and information to unfold for me, and it all led me to where I am now and the writing of this book.

Everyone has a story and literally, anyone could take their lives and the experiences of living it and turn them into a book. Some people do and some people don't. A lot of times, the content put out from those who decided to share by writing, serves to help, in some form or fashion, some of those who have read or will read the book. So the writing of their story and turning it into a book that others could read, resonate with and learn from, is helping the world to some degree, one reader at a time.

I am writing a book telling readers of my story and showing them some of the techniques I used to help myself through the hurdles and obstacles that I've faced over the years, with the hopes that it will help someone who may have experienced or who is in the midst of experiencing something similar.

Most especially with this last rock bottom event that I experienced because it became my game changer. Maybe someone who can relate or with whom my story resonates with will pick this book up right in the moment when it's needed the most. I am writing a book without any book writing experience, a bunch of degrees or a specialty in some field that I have mastered successfully.

However, I am writing a book about something that I know everything about, and that would be my life, of which I am an expert. I've experienced a lot in this life, some of which I share with you. Consider this my testimony all packaged up nice and neat into a book! I choose to share my life experiences and how I overcame any obstacles faced so that I could build myself back up, in the hopes that it can help someone.

Ordinary people can do extraordinary things when they get out of their way.

INVICTUS

"Out of the night that covers me,
Black as the Pit from pole to pole,
I thank whatever gods may be
For my unconquerable soul.

In the fell clutch of circumstance
I have not winced nor cried aloud.
Under the bludgeoning of chance
My head is bloody, but unbowed.

Beyond this place of wrath and tears
Looms but the Horror of the shade
And yet the menace of the years
Finds, and shall find, me unafraid.

It matters not how strait the gate
How charged with punishments the scroll.
I am the master of my fate
I am the captain of my soul."

Invictus (1875)
William Ernest Henley (1849-1903)
(Book of Verses)

CHAPTER 1

Unconscious Behavior

Every day, in every moment we are making choices, deciding what to do. On a daily basis, from the moment you feel yourself become consciously awake, you are making decisions that affect you and the world around you. Please think about that for a moment. You roll over in bed. You may hit the snooze button or lay there awake but unmoving. You think about whether you should get up and use the bathroom, or get a cup of coffee or tea. Maybe go straight to getting ready for the day. Perhaps you're running your agenda through your mind, planning out your day; you get the point.

We do these things, habitually, without even having to think about it. We're thinking, but we do not have to focus on thinking. We're not confused by having to decide. We know what needs to happen and, for the most part, we do it. That is, we'll execute some form of action by making a conscious decision subconsciously.

See, by the time you go to act on a decision, you've already determined your choice in your mind. Every decision that we make is because we have options, opportunities, and the ability to choose. Otherwise, there'd be no need for deciding on anything. You'd merely be operating without free will, performing whatever function(s) you were programmed to do. However, we enter this earth with the privilege of free will and are therefore subject to decision making daily. We put into place these routines that are basically structured or chaotic habits, and we operate accordingly, subconsciously.

21

Every single action you take started first as an idea in your mind of which you made a decision about. If, for example, you decided you would not get out of the bed for the day, for whatever reason, you've <u>decided</u> to <u>choose</u> to take that particular <u>action</u>. How we use this to our advantage and take control of this unconscious behavior is by first recognizing that this is so. Accepting what it is and the effect that it's having on your life in the now and then deciding to do something about it based on whether or not you like where you are in your life and where you are aiming to go.

Let's assume for the purposes of this book, that you are currently reading this because you are seeking ways to improve your life. I should mention that it's my belief, that we are, as human beings, always growing and evolving and that there is always room for improvement. Either way, you can learn something from this book or confirm and therefore reinforce some things you already know by reading this book, and then it would be up to you to implement it.

So in using this to your advantage, you are going to take control of that unconscious behavior by getting to the core of what it is that you want. You'll be outlining how you'd want to process and act on those wants; and then dictating to your subconscious, a new pattern of behaviors, by creating new habits that you will act on subconsciously, implementing decisions that you've actioned on consciously.

Let's stop right here and assess some things before going further. F.Y.I, you're going to need a dedicated notebook if you're serious about doing this, so please have your pen and notebook ready when working from this book. You can also purchase The Decision Workbook which already has the worksheets outlined for you and goes a little further to help you break down the answers to these questions which ultimately will help you to compose a completed Goal and Action Plan for your life over the next 7-10 years.

Please answer these questions in as detailed a manner as you can, being totally honest with yourself. Then I want you to go back over your answers and highlight every instance where you were either being too lenient with your truths or too harsh on yourself. We're all subject to this, so go on ahead and do it.

1. Are you happy with your life as it is right now?
2. Why or why not?
3. What are some steps you can take right now to improve your life no matter what your life's circumstances are?
4. How would you go about taking these steps?
5. Now go back over the answers to questions #3 & 4 and list every obstacle that came to mind as you were writing your answers.
6. Now list what it would take to remove those obstacles.
7. What can you do, according to the list from question #6, to jumpstart removing the obstacles that you believe are keeping you from taking the steps needed to improve your life's circumstances?
8. Now list the first 3 actionable steps that you will take to get started on improving your life's circumstances in the now.

Pretty simple, wouldn't you say? Well, I wouldn't say it was simple. In fact, I didn't find it to be simple at all. The questions are meant to go deep, and it immediately caused my brain to go into "freeze" or "pause" mode, from the thought of the work involved with answering the first two questions alone. All I saw was A LOT of work! Most especially when your life is seemingly a chaotic abyss! Also, because laziness can come running just as soon as you're faced with having to do something you don't necessarily care to do. It did for me at least. I speak from experience. Not that you don't want to have it done; only that you don't care to be the one doing it.

In my mind, I can hear my Grandmother saying as I'm typing this, "Get your lazy ass up and get to work!" Bless her soul. She's gone now, but no doubt has left a lasting impression on me. Her description of me, however, was accurate. I did indeed have a tendency towards laziness that followed me into my adult life. Yes, I worked, took care of the household and the children, but never at my highest and best capacity. I was a servant of mediocrity, doing just enough to get by. Sure, it looked good from the outside looking in, but it was no-where near what I was truly capable of. In hindsight, I was allowing all of that potential to squander away. All because I didn't want to have to do more than was required to get by.

Getting back to the laziness, I believe it's essential to address the elephant in the room. There's quite a bit of chatter going on about motivation, faith, changing your life, building stamina and belief in yourself, but let's face it, some people genuinely are just lazy. They have the know-how, the tools and resources, the capabilities and some are even living life by way of silver platters; Still, they're lazy and don't want to do the work it takes to live as a successfully productive citizen in our society!

Not that some of them aren't working or contributing in some form or fashion to society as a whole, but that they could knowingly be doing more to improve the quality of their lives and those around them, but they are consciously choosing not to. Whether they have been conditioned to believe and live this way, by life's circumstances and situations or not, they are still droning through life. You may be one of these people that I am addressing. Eliminate your thoughts of being offended right at this moment! You can't get caught up in your feelings at a time such as this.

What would be the point in going through this, if you're not going to get down to the nitty-gritty of things? It's in those deep, soul-searching questions that you're going to find your core reasons behind why you do some of the things you are currently doing in your life anyway! For some of us, laziness has been playing a significant part in our lives! So now you have to decide. Will you take the time to do the work? Are you going to be truthful and honest with yourself? If you believe you lack the time needed to do the work, are you willing to *make* the required time? Can you dedicate yourself to improving your life so that you can finally be what you've always wanted it to be? Are you ready to live in your greatness?

After all, droning through life is just going through the motions to get by. Sometimes we don't realize that we're even doing this because we've experienced the repetitive cycle of going through something and barely making it through on so many different occasions, that we've gotten used to being happy with just barely making it through, but never rising above it. That's what conditioning is. It's being exposed to something so much so, that it changes your behavior to conform to the exposure. You began to normalize what you're experiencing and feeling from that exposure, and a subconscious coping mechanism clicks and kicks in, making you think and believe that you've overcome something when in truth, you're just numb to it. Either way, you're still living, working, interacting with friends and family. Like a shell. An empty shell with no feeling. You're just droning, but today is a new day! You've made a decision that, if taken seriously, should alter the course of your life!

Commit to having an actionable response to the excuses that will inevitably come up as you are working to live in your greatness! Map out a measurable plan that will lead you to the life you are wanting to live using realistic and attainable goals. Let us consciously begin to restructure that unconscious behavior. Roll up your sleeves and let's do this!

CHAPTER 2

The Purge, The Mourning & The Yellow Brick Road

There used to be a time when I didn't like being alone with my thoughts. Now, however, while it can still get uncomfortable, I'm willing to let those uncomfortable thoughts run through my mind. By allowing my thoughts to run their course, it's been helping me to self-evaluate some things about myself and my way of thinking. This has helped me to separate fact from fiction, truth from lies and process past incidents that have stayed with me all of these years. In this way, I've been processing some things to properly put them in their place and purging through others that needed to be laid to rest.

Mourning affords us the opportunity to process and release our pain, disappointment and hurt. A true mourning will, in the end, provide a sense of relief; possibly even a sense of freedom. All of which depends on the individual. No two people will process the same and some will need more time than others. I've been allowing myself the time to mourn by taking the necessary time to release emotionally. This usually requires me to pull back from everyone so that the only chatter in my ear is that of my own. Anytime I've genuinely given myself the room to fully mourn the loss of something or someone important to me, I've been able to put it in my past for good. I'm of the mindset that recurring thoughts of past hurt, pain, and disappointment comes from unresolved issues surrounding those thoughts. If you are truly seeking to let go of anything or anyone that has caused you any hurt, pain or disappointment, and you are ready to move on with your life, the mourning process will most certainly be a part of your healing.

You'll need the cousins, faith and belief, in order to truly follow this path that you have chosen to embark on. You see faith and belief, while closely related, are not the same; but for sure, are a duo that you'd best have in your repertoire if you genuinely want to accomplish everything you've just planned out in the previous chapters. Faith and belief strengthen and aid in reinforcing the other. A journey without faith and belief is no journey at all. Faith inspires us to press on and continue forward while belief gives you the confidence to follow that inspiration. This is where the yellow brick road comes into play. Following the path of the yellow brick road is all about faith and belief. Having the faith that what you're seeking is at the end of that road, and believing that you are capable of making the journey. Along the way, you build your strength, courage, and knowledge. You may find yourself letting go of some folks and meeting new people who add value to your life; gaining a little wisdom even.

If I had to sum up the meaning of this chapter, the purge, the mourning, and the yellow brick road, I'd say this is where you are making the room that's necessary for your life to grow.

The Purge

The purging process isn't necessarily the easiest to go through, but it is a necessary one. Some of us would rather deal with the pain of a problem using some form of coping mechanism to get by, rather than having to deal with the pain of getting to the root of a problem in order to eliminate it for good. It's better to get to the "deep-seeded" root of a problem and cut it off or repair it from the point of entry or inception. Rather than attempting to quick fix it by covering it up or "packing it away" and ignoring it in the hopes that it would just disappear, so that you didn't have to deal with the emotional pain that can come with purging. There is an inner clearing within yourself and an invisible weight that is lifted when you have properly processed any event or problem in your life that has caused you to pause or that has created a glitch in your flow.

The Purging process is about getting rid of something, but you can't get rid of what you don't or can't see. I'm asking you to seek out the root of the problem by stripping away the layers. Getting to the reason the problem even exists; to handle *that* by dealing with it head-on to keep from repeating it over and over again. The process of purging requires that you go deep. Everything that happens to you, good or bad, leads back to a decision or choice that you've made that has led to what you're experiencing, good or bad.

So if you're finding yourself experiencing an undesirable recurring problem in your life, then I'm going to need you to go all the way back to square one to figure out where it is along this path, that things started to get crooked.

The Mourning

Allow yourself the time to mourn properly. You've got to take the time to get it off of your chest, out of your system and off your mind. Just don't get stuck there! You've got to have a snap-back plan even when you believe there is nothing and no-one to grasp on to. After all, nothing and no-one can compel you to do something for yourself, save for you. Most especially when you lack the motivation even to breathe.

I'm aware of the mindset of some people who believe it best to just put your big girl panties on and get on with life. It happened, it hurt you, now move on. Shouldn't you be over this by now? Why are you holding on to the past? You're weak minded because you won't let go and more statements of the like; you get the point.

However, I believe that proper mourning allows you to move on free and clear because your "system" won't continuously break down every time there's a reminder of whatever it is that has caused the glitch in your flow. Resetting your way of thinking (your mindset) in regards to whom or what you lost will aid you in being able to go forward with your life in an emotionally healthy state that will be conducive to your future. In this way, you go forward carrying no baggage in tow from whatever situation you've processed through.

There is nothing like a good dose of wallowing in your sorrow to help you on your way. You have to remember to approach and enter this period of mourning as part of your action plan to moving forward with your life. Mourning periods will vary by the individual, but the intent and purpose of the grieving should be the same all around, and that is to move on with your life free and clear. So again I remind you, don't get stuck!

The questions you should have completed in chapter one are intended to give you a point of starting in this process; but also an anchor in which you can use to stand firm. By the end of that assignment, you should have come out of it with mini action plans that YOU decided on to help you work towards living in your greatness!

The Yellow Brick Road

It's ok if you can't see the entire picture or all the way to the other side of your sorrows while in mourning. Trust the process and continue to press on because every step you complete opens up a more precise view of the next level or actions that you'll need to take. Your true freedom is on the other end, and this will become clearer to you as you go along. Even Dorothy, from the iconic classic The Wiz, couldn't see the whole yellow brick road, but she trusted that at the end of each part she made it through, more of said road would be there for her to follow. Every obstacle that she faced while traveling along this road made her stronger for the end of her journey. It fortified her inner strength and allowed her to be a source of strength for her companions even as she was working through her fears and disappointments. She'd conquered so many obstacles along the way, that by the time she reached the end of that yellow brick road, she was a force to be reckoned with! In the end, what Dorothy thought she was seeking at the end of the yellow brick road, she found, was with her all along!

Your journey is not just about you. This will become clearer to you as you go along. It's not about you. It's bigger than you! By the time you've completed this process, not only will you have found that what you needed was there, within you, all along; but you'll also help some of those around you, who you will inspire simply because they were watching you! Chew on that as we go into the next segment.

CHAPTER 3

Acceptance & Responsibility

Ok, so now that we have clear and concise answers to the questions that were presented in chapter one, we will begin to work through them so that each response can be processed. Remember, the only way to truly live in your greatness is to earnestly work through the core issues that may have been holding you back consciously or subconsciously throughout the years.

Without even knowing that our circumstances have programmed us, you may have been droning through life operating with the subtly embedded idea imprinted in you that tells you that you are unworthy or undeserving of success. Success in this instance is defined as "the accomplishment of an aim or purpose." Your past is not allowing you to live honey bunches, so we're about to fix all of that!

1. **How many questions from chapter one did you answer in the moment?**
2. **What did you learn about yourself that you may not have paid attention to before now?**

The questions posed to you in chapter one were the openers for the foundational questions. The questions that will have you peering into your very soul for answers. Who will you be working on if you don't know who you are? You need to be transparent about the real you, flaws and all. There's no need to reveal it to anyone. This exercise is for you. You want a good look at who you really are. What you're really like? The good, bad and ugly; every facet of your ego broken down until there's nothing left there but you.

3. **So who are you really?** Please be as detailed as possible and know that it may not be so easy to admit some truths about yourself; but remember, this exercise is for YOU!

_____
_____
_____
_____
_____
_____
_____
_____
_____
_____

We are talking about acceptance and responsibility. Once you get down to the nitty-gritty of who you are and can see it and admit it to yourself, you'll need to accept that this is who you are and take responsibility for who you've been thus far. You needn't worry about being this way in the future because from this point on; you'll be taking control of your life from your ego by putting your foot down, so to speak. From this point on, now that you know who you really are, who you've been up until now, and you have accepted that this is who you've been; you'll have to decide on whether or not you like who you are and who you have been up to this point. Taking full responsibility for being that person, operate with deliberate intent to become the person you want to be if you're not already living this way.

4. **Who do you want to be? What do you want to be in this life?**

_____
_____
_____
_____
_____

Acceptance may come with having to chew that pill that's not so easily swallowed. What doesn't kill you should only help you to grow right?

5. **Taking the answers from question #7 in chapter one, what of those answers, if any, can you use to apply to question #4 here in chapter 3?**

_____
_____
_____

(You should refer to your workbook or notebook for easy access to the questions already answered.)

If you've found that none of the answers given from #7 chapter 1 will work on helping you to achieve the answers you've given for #4 chapter 3, you may have some re-evaluating to do.

While there are no right or wrong answers here, there can be superficial answers which will be washed away with the first sign of doubt because they hold no real weight; or there will be more meaningful answers that can substantially impact the actionable responses to any obstacles that may arise. It is those type of answers that will become your go-to mechanism for handling barriers as they appear. The goal here is not to stroke your ego but, instead, to find solutions to your obstacles.

Now, taking all of this new information gathered during the exercises, list three things that you will do immediately to get started on working towards who and what you want to be in this life. Then do it!

_____
_____
_____

In doing these exercises, answering these questions and mapping out actionable responses to them, you are in effect, creating a series of short-term action plans that will allow you to measure and celebrate your mini-successes and milestones. You are outlining both your short and your long-term goals because these exercises inevitably lead you to that end result.

By giving serious thought to and then faithfully acting on your actionables, you are now enforcing discipline to successfully complete the tasks. That's empowering in and of itself! These small action plans will lend themselves to the bigger picture, and because of the mini successes, you'll feel all the more empowered to meet the goals of your three, five and seven-year plans.

Remember, no matter what others hold on to from your past, **you are not your past!** Your result, who you are now, is a product of your history. It does not define you; it only adds to enhance who you are. It's because of your past that you've been able to grow in the manner that you have. No one can define this for you and for sure they cannot take it from you!

CHAPTER 4

Execution: How to Execute with Immediate Results by Taking Action in the Moment

You've made The Decision; that's great, beautiful and wonderful! You've done some soul searching and you have created some action plans. Now it's time to put those plans in motion by getting started on those life-changing actionables (my terminology) that you've come up with during your exercises!

In fact, by the time you reach this chapter, you should have already knocked out quite a few actionables. That's how the previous chapters were designed. There should be no scenario what so ever where you have not completed any actionables as of yet. Otherwise, you might as well put this book down now. Or better yet, give it to someone you don't like. You're not ready.

On the other hand, you may very well be psyched up about this new path you've chosen to embark on and even looking forward to what's to come once your plan(s) have been implemented. However, you may still find yourself at a crossroads of knowing what you want to do, but not exactly knowing *how* to get jumpstarted into *actually* doing it. Trust me when I say that I'm speaking from experience.

Most any and everything that I can talk about stems solely from my experience, and it's strictly from my perspective; my point of view. So it's always one-sided thoughts or words, carefully put together and shared with others, in the hopes that my experiences can be of help to someone who may be trying to navigate through this string of moment points, we call life, here on this earth.

As simple as it may sound, it's not always easy to move from *wanting* to do something to *actually* getting it done. For me, I was constantly finding myself stuck on the "how." There's so much good advice out there from people who were willing to share their experiences and what worked for them while working towards living their version of a successful life. Some of which is self-explanatory. Some, of which, would only apply to *their* individual circumstances and some of which lacked a very simple *how* in making it happen.

The Giraffe and the Turtle

The giraffe can tell that turtle everything that it sees, and the turtle can imagine everything the giraffe is telling him about what he sees, but he's still limited in how he can perceive it because he only knows the view from his level; his perspective. He can only see things from his point of view.

There is a solution, however, in helping the turtle to see better what's being described from the giraffe's point of view. The giraffe could simply lift the turtle up, or the turtle could climb up on the giraffe to get a better view. The turtle, after all, is the one who has to *want* to be able to see things from this other point of view. However, it would still involve the giraffe being *willing* to assist the turtle in being able to see things from the giraffes' point of view. In this case, the giraffe can assist by either lifting the turtle or allowing the turtle to climb up on the giraffes' back, to get a better point of view. In doing this, the turtle can now see things from a different perspective. Taking this newfound view he's received, he'll now be able to apply what he's learned, to living life at his level. By broadening his perspective, being shown a new connection to all things, the turtle can now live a more prosperous life down in his world, because he would have learned of new ways to navigate through it.

During my studies and while I was in a period of seeking and searching for myself, I did a lot of reading, researching and video watching trying to elevate myself. I had to find mentors whose "talk-speak" resonated with me and of whose mindset and lives were already in a place of which I was aiming to go. I was now seeking answers and solutions to overcoming my obstacles, motivating myself and acquiring the knowledge and skills needed in order to live in my greatness.

I came across a book called *The 5 Second Rule* by *Mel Robbins*. Motivation being for the birds from her point of view, the very core of her book is about how you can trick your mind into taking action by jumpstarting it with a countdown. This method applies to any and as many actions throughout any given day, as needed. The idea being that you would spring into action immediately following your countdown and accomplish whatever task(s) you needed to complete.

I modified the basis of this principle for myself and applied it in a way that fit my situation. Taking into account the level of my will power, the level of my self-discipline and my ability to see things through, I made the necessary changes to suit my individual needs, in order to have the successful outcome that I was aiming for. Every little conquest strengthens you for the next, and I believe that this method is an absolute awesome way to jumpstart your day and to help you get your work done, no matter the task. What was most important for me with her method, was the "how." It wasn't just an idea of what to do. It was also the "how" to do it factor.

You can do anything you want to do if you just know how to do it. When you don't know how you should be seeking the answer to that very question. How? How do I get there? How do I do this or that? How can I make this happen? How can I implement this in my life? I don't believe that human beings are filled with a desire to do anything that they are incapable of doing, as we all come with our specific specialty skillset for living this life. Therefore you *can* do *anything* you want to do *if* you know how to go about doing it. Period!

I do believe, however, that you must know yourself. Knowing and understanding your strengths and weaknesses in order to keep honest with yourself at all times, will enable you to be better equipped to make the change(s) that you've decided you'll be making in your life and for yourself. However, some people struggle with discipline and prioritizing. Some folks get caught up and stuck in deciding, only to end up getting nothing done. Some folks don't have the skill of discipline that it takes to enforce the "blast off" at the end of the countdown. Therefore, assessing your strengths and weaknesses, for the purpose, of keeping honest with yourself, is crucial to this critical moment in your life of redefining yourself.

We human beings are individuals who don't all operate on the same level. Don't worry about or compare yourself to others. Do not allow yourself to feed into being judged by others. As you also most certainly should be mindful of refraining from the act of judging others. "Judge not lest ye be judged" (Matthew 7:1 KJV). The bible is filled with common sense advice. It's not your right to tell people where they should or need to be. If you disagree with this statement, then ask yourself this, whose right is it to tell you where you should or need to be? Who's responsible for telling *you* how to lead *your* life?

You create your system in earnest and with specificity to work for you. Essentially, what's important here is that you begin taking control of how your life is constructed, by taking the steps, little by little, that are outlined in your plans. You have created a series of mini plans geared towards reconstructing your life to that which you desire it to be, and you are now operating with intention in every single move you make! If you bump into a "how" block, then take the necessary moment you need to learn, understand and then implement it in your plan.

If you've completed the exercises from the previous chapters thus far, then at this point you are doing what you *must* do to make things happen and get the outcome(s) that you desire. **You are the boss of you** at any given time! Do what you have to do to make it through any uncomfortable moments that may arise while you're snatching back control of your life. Once you process through those awkward and, at times, painful moments, you take back the control over your life.

Through *my* processing, I have determined that this world is not my own. It's the reason why I've never fit in and why no matter the setting, I always seemed to be the outsider. That is until I decided that I would no longer allow that to be the case anymore! I did this by figuring out my "how." It was time for me to take over how this life was going for me and take charge of the direction(s) in which my life flowed. Now that I have fully processed my thoughts surrounding fitting in, I am free and clear of what was holding me back from expanding in my life in that way. Now my belief is, whether I am of this world or not, *I live here*; therefore it is. I fit in, any and everywhere I go because I say so and I act accordingly! I now operate according to this belief; Point, blank, period.

Perception and discipline play strong, critical roles in our lives. How we see the situations and circumstances in our lives determine how we act or react to those situations and circumstances that is our lives. This would apply to all that we consider to be good in our lives, as well as what we believe to be bad or wrong in or about our lives. Perception is unique to the individual. It is the way that we receive and process incoming information and communication, from the world around us; and how we perceive it, determines how we respond to it.

You have to be able to self-ignite that sense of urgency within yourself when carrying out the goals that you've set. You need the ability to jumpstart yourself into being able to carry out your everyday remedial tasks. You need to hone in on those skills such as prioritizing and organizing that will aid you in successfully being able to accomplish your goals. You need a system designed just for you utilizing your God-given specialty skillset!

Discipline is a skill. The good news here is that if you lack it, you *can* have it. You have to want it though. Discipline is the tool you'll use to make yourself do a task even when you're not feeling up to doing it. Discipline will help you accomplish a great many of your goals if you use it. It's a skill that's used as a tool! Get yourself some!

Let's assess your level of procrastination. Keeping it real, everyone has a bit of it, somewhere, within us. You can do this by giving a more in-depth look at the tasks you consider or perceive to be important or unimportant in your day-to-day activities. Create yourself a list and use it to determine where the breakdown in communication happens; between knowing what you need to do and getting those things done. This list will consist of the tasks you like to do, those you don't mind doing and those things you put off until you have no choice but to do it. Things that you choose to choose to ignore or leave undone.

With the completion of this list, you'll be able to pinpoint your peak points of procrastination and target the tasks that are more likely to cause you to pause. With this information, you are going to formulate a plan, specific to you and how you operate, that will allow you to accomplish all of your everyday tasks and meet your daily goals.

The goal here is to put into place a process that works best in switching your gears into action mode. We can write a thousand "to do" lists. Make a thousand different plans. Go over our goals again and again until they're some un-abided law in our minds. None of that will make any difference nor contribute to the betterment of your life if you don't do anything about it! If you are having trouble in this area you need to be asking yourself:

- **Do you believe in yourself? Why or why not?**
- **Do you believe in the goals that you've set thus far? Why or why not?**
- **Do you believe your goals are realistic? Attainable? Why or why not?**
- **Do you believe yourself capable of carrying out those goals? Why or why not?**
- **What's *truly* stopping you from moving forward in your life?**

Be honest with yourself! Do yourself a favor and choose not to hurry your way through these questions by giving superficial answers. Seriously! No one's looking. If you can't be honest with yourself then . . .

Listen, the outcome that you're looking for, if achieved, will lift you higher and bring more to your life. More emotionally, possibly physically, materialistically, and for sure more responsibility. Without a doubt, you *will* increase the quality of your life. Try to remember that every experience in our string of moment points is a lesson to be learned. This reasoning is why it's so important to build yourself up on a firm foundation — keeping it real with *yourself* 100% of the time from the very beginning of embarking on this journey. In this way, you are less likely to suffer from failing, falling and watching your world crumble around you.

If you do fall, however, you should keep in mind that the more you have, the harder your fall; and the hardest part about falling so hard is *believing* that you have the ability to snap back from it and get yourself up and going again.

It's not impossible. You *can* build yourself back up again! You have everything you need within you to succeed at ANYTHING you *genuinely* want to do. So ask yourself, if you find that you're still stuck by the time you reach this chapter, what is it that you GENUINELY want to do? Only YOU will know this for sure.

Make that decision today! Right now! In *this* moment! Feel it! Feel it so deep in you that it tingles in your toes. Feel it so deep in you that you can feel that tingle working its way up to your heart and mind. That tingle is your belief; and as we all well know by now, we can do ANYTHING we BELIEVE is possible!

CHAPTER 5

When You're Tired of Mastering Mediocrity

MEDIOCRITY - plural mediocrities
The quality or state of being mediocre
Moderate ability or value
MEDIOCRE - Of moderate or low quality, value, ability, or performance:
ORDINARY, SO-SO
*https://www.merriam-webster.com/dictionary/mediocre

The path that we are to follow on this journey that we chose to partake in isn't always easy, happy or fun. Yet the majority of us that are here on our journeys continue to press on in light of and in spite of the trials, tribulations, disappointments, setbacks, and heartache that we face. You may have wondered, asked even, why you were purposed with a mission such as this. Seeking a deeper meaning to life because surely this couldn't be it?!

If you find yourself relating to that passage, I want you to answer these questions for yourself.

- ❖ **Why do you feel like you can relate to this passage?**
- ❖ **What parts of your life lead you to feel unsure of your purpose in this lifetime?**

- ❖ **Why do you continue to press on in spite of the trials, tribulations, and disappointments?**
- ❖ **What satisfaction, if any, do you gain from continuing to press on despite the hardships?**
- ❖ **Why do you believe you have been experiencing these hardships throughout your life?**

Please be sure to think about and write a thorough answer for each question. You have the ability to do so, and in doing so, you will begin to see the areas of mediocre expertise you've mastered throughout your life.

Belief in yourself made easier by the successes, big and small, throughout your life that made you *feel* validated. Accolades from others in and around your life that you deemed important because silently you seek approval from them. The constant living in judgment of yourself because of the ever going comparison of yourself against the others in and around your life.

Mediocrity simmers at the baseline of our lives because it works in direct correlation with self-esteem; specifically, low self-esteem.

How many times throughout your life have you heard it said that you could be and do anything you want to be or do in life? If you're anything like me, you've listened to this regularly from one adult or other in your life, throughout your childhood. Likewise, if you think about it, you may have even repeated these same words to a good many of the children who you've come across in the past as well as those in your present life. How many times have you repeated these words to another adult in your life? How many times has another adult come to you and tried to encourage you using that same statement?

Immediately you should be able to see how easily these habits of encouraging a child about the possibilities the world has to offer them and how the sky has *no* limit, at some point drifts away when we reach a certain age in our young adulthood. No specific age to define, but if you think back, the

majority of us will note that at some point, all of a sudden the sky *was* the limit.

You are faking the funk until you can make it and being good at it to boot! Only to realize that you've faked the funk for so long that you never bothered, to actually get to the point of making it. As long as you kept receiving those pats on the back, you had no reason to believe you needed to do anything more!

When you find yourself just doing enough to get by, you are living a mediocre life! Not because you can't do more or better with yourself. Not because you are limited in your ability to do more or better with yourself. More so because you have become *comfortable* with doing a *superb* job at living at or below average and doing so because to the outsider looking in, you'd appear to be "doing well." To do anything else, would require too much effort on your part. This statement applies to anybody no matter their walk or stature in life. There is *ALWAYS* room for improvement in your life! Some, maybe more than others, and the areas of mediocrity will vary, but most certainly this applies to everyone.

The first change that you are to make in eliminating mediocrity out of your life is to remove any barriers between you, where you are right at this moment, and where you are trying to go! That means you are about to make an executive decision to toss out any and every excuse you have utilized, thus far, to this point in your life.

This IS NOT a "do it later" chapter! You MUST do this now!

Take a deep breath, suck it ALL in . . . And release. You have to feel this in every fiber of your being because everything you seek will come to you through this feeling. I CANNOT stress that enough! Also, if you lack belief in this process, then you're wasting your time!

More important than believing in this process is believing in yourself. When you start to question your reasoning for half stepping, you open the door to rooting out why it is that you're *choosing* not to give your all or do your best in the areas of your life where you've mastered mediocrity. You will be calling your bluff and inevitably coming face to face with the deep to the core truth about the fact that you haven't been living as your Optimal You.

Once again, these exercises are for YOU. PLEASE DO NOT CHEAT YOURSELF. If I come across as repetitive, it's because I know and understand how important it is, especially during a time such as this. When you are stripping away every façade used in your life to create and live as the person you've been up until now, you want to have the reassurance that you can go that deep and you *will* be ok. One of the greater satisfactions out of life is having a lightbulb come on when you've been in the dark for so long. That's self-gratification! You are doing something that will ultimately be pleasing to you, but even better than that; it will lead to a new and improved you! That's empowering all on its own.

Before moving on to the next chapter, take the time needed to complete each question posed above. You'll give yourself some much-needed clarity. This clarity will enable you to continue building towards a solid foundation for your new beginning.

"Nothing shall come to pass, until everything is In Its Place"

I can see her standing there you know. By her, I mean me. I can see myself standing there in a distant, yet familiar land; deserted looking, yet full of life. There are mounds of sand hills and the sun is shining bright. Enough so, that I'm finding that I'm having to wince just to be able to see, yet I'm not hot. I can hear the wind blowing, but the sand isn't moving and I cannot feel a breeze.

I know I must begin my journey and I'm filled with thoughts and questions about what the journey will entail. I'm feeling excited, frustrated and slightly afraid of what's to come, because at this point, it's all unknown to me.

Armed with everything I will need, yet not carrying a thing, I take a deep breath and I begin my journey one step at a time, while this song the length of one sentence plays over and over in my heart. Nothing shall come to pass, until everything is in its place.

#LetTheJourneyBegin

CHAPTER 6

Going Before the Judges

Let me share with you the response of someone, of whom I held in high regard when I went to this person as a source of strength while I was in the midst of going through that horrible time in my life. I want you to have an understanding of how much power we give to others when we begin to value their opinions above our own. In my last encounter with this person, their reaction to what I had to say as I was explaining the situation and what I was going through, was from the point of judgment. Keep in mind that I was very emotional but coherent and in control. I'd had a lot I needed to get off of my chest and I was seeking the advice of someone more experienced than myself, who I believed could offer me words of encouragement, a voice of reason and perhaps even some actionable advice.

People have a tendency to judge you based off of your past and not for who you are in the now. All of the steps that you've taken to become who you are now; the trials and the tribulations you've made it through, the ups and the downs you went through, that make you who you are now, matters not to a person who can't see past your past. Everything it took to grow into who you are now is of no concern to them. It's neither here nor there at the end of the day because who is any one person, to judge another? No one on the face of this earth has the right to judge another. As if they, themselves, are above being judged.

To judge someone is to impose upon them, your opinion(s) about their behaviors, words, and actions. It is the expression of an opinion about the above stated and then coming to a conclusion based off of your opinion about those things. Whether the opinion is to make a note of something good or something not so great, it's still an opinion based off of your perception of the person. That perception is then compared to your experiences and beliefs. Therefore, judgment is not about the person being judged, but more so about the person doing the judging.

For example, someone does something you consider to be good, and you're saying to them "Oh you did so well! You did such a good job! I'm so proud of you!" In your *opinion*, that person did well. In your *opinion*, you believe that they took the right steps and made the right moves and that made *you* proud, and it made *you* feel good. Your judgment of them was favorable, or so it would appear.

Nevertheless, you still judged them. You can genuinely be happy or sad for someone, disappointed in or angry with someone, but it's not your place to judge another. By doing so, you place yourself in the position of God and law over the life of another when you choose to judge them.

Hear this and take it to heart. Another person's opinion of you does not matter to you; it shouldn't anyway because it has nothing to do with you. It's all about them! Their lives, their experiences, their ways of thinking, their thoughts and actions help them to compose opinions about what the life, thoughts, activities, and words of another should also be. It's solely on them. It has nothing to do with you. That being said, no one should be walking around judging you; but even if they choose to, who cares? What difference does it make to you? It's really none of your business!

There used to be a time when other people's opinion of me mattered more to me than that of my own. I based my life off of how others thought I should be living it — the things I should be doing. The way I should be carrying myself. The way I should be speaking. My words, actions, and behaviors were made from a place of wanting to impress others. Once upon a time, I wouldn't make a move in my life without first consulting someone about it. Consulting with one person or another in my life, whose opinion I valued over my own, about something I wanted to do, was doing or I'd already done.

My life was run by other people. What they thought I should be doing. How they thought I should be living, speaking, working and carrying out my day-to-day. Everything I did was based on the opinions of others. I was giving away my power daily until I learned to trust and believe in myself. Now, the thoughts and opinions of others regarding my life and how I'm living is of no concern to me. I recognize that it's a reflection of them and therefore none of my business.

Basically, in viewing and listening to this person respond to me from the point of judgment, I decided right at that moment not to take their responses to heart and that perhaps, at least for now, our time in this life had come to a close. It was the ending of a chapter in our lives together. When a person in your life cannot see past your past, perhaps a break is necessary. Growth and evolution is an inevitable occurrence amongst us humans. Maybe we'll have another chapter together later on in this life.

If you are looking to successfully change your life with this decision that you have made, trust and belief in yourself is an absolute requirement. No matter what it is that you are doing in and with your life, you should be trusting and believing in yourself! Why boggle yourself down with the negative thoughts and opinions of others? Even in the case of a favorable impression, judgment is still judgment. Right? Kudos to them if they feel good about you and the life that you've lived or the things that you've done. Whether the opinions of others are favorable or not, you should be feeling good about yourself. You should carry your strength within you! That strength is drawn from your trust and belief in yourself!

Your opinion of yourself, the way you choose to judge yourself, the level of standards to which you hold yourself, that's the only judgment that matters. It's the sole judgment that should have you take a more in-depth look at yourself; and of course, it should go without saying, you can't be capable of holding yourself in high esteem when you don't trust and believe in yourself! If you're suffering from low self-esteem, you'll need to address it in the now! Nothing you plan or map out can work for you if you don't believe yourself capable of successfully doing so.

Concerning going before the judges, only you can measure your success in life. Only you know how much you've grown from who and where you were and who and where you want to be. You're the executor of your life! People can and *will* give you their opinions, invited or not. Your job is to remember that their opinion is just that . . . an opinion. It's not law. It does not define you. You can pull from it what you want and toss every other part of it away. Remember not to get caught up in your feelings about the words and thoughts of others, but pay attention to anything that sparks an emotion, of any kind, within you.

We're human beings. We're not perfect. We'll do and say some things that we may wish we had an opportunity to do or say differently. Things that may have had a detrimental impact on our lives and maybe that of the lives of some of the folks that are or were in our circle. No one can change what has already happened. You shouldn't walk around condemning yourself to the point where you can't live because of past mistakes, words, and decisions. Likewise, do not allow others to condemn you.

You want to be consciously aware of the ease in which it is to judge the actions of another. In the same way that you don't want to be judged, you also don't want to go around passing judgment on others. Your opinions, choices, and beliefs have nothing to do with someone else. It's more than likely something that you would do for yourself. When sharing your opinions and thoughts with another, try to remember not to judge them for the choices that they make. Ultimately, it's up to the individual to decide on the fate of their lives. It's not our place to interfere. This especially makes me think of rearing children. We raise them according to our beliefs. We guide them in the best way we know how and when they become of age and start expressing their individuality; we find ourselves comparing and measuring their actions to our beliefs; judging them.

We don't want them to make the mistakes that we've made. We try our best to lead them towards the path that we hope they'll be the most successful. If you are to believe that everything happens for a reason (and I do), then even when we don't like or agree with the choices our children are making, we should carry hope in the fact that they are in the midst of experiencing some life lessons that are preparing them for *their* purpose in this life.

Let's not judge others for choosing a path other than the one we would have them to take. We do it so often without even thinking about it that it will take a conscious effort until the habit is fully formed. Likewise, be mindful of changing your behavior, thoughts or decisions to suit another's beliefs. This practice will embed itself in you if used enough; so start now.

Eventually, you'll notice how light you feel not having to carry the weight of pressure put on you by the opinions of others. Standing firm in who you are, with confidence — knowing that you are living in the freedom of your individuality. Your chest should be puffing out like you have a big 'ole "S" on it. Own it!

CHAPTER 7

Holding On While Letting Go - The Law of Detachment

"You must find the place inside yourself where nothing is impossible."
--- Deepak Chopra

'For it's in the impossible, that you will find everything.'
--- Mecheline Muhammad

The Law of Detachment isn't really a law. It's more of a philosophic view on life and how keeping detached allows us to participate, more fully, in the world while at the same time, operating outside of the limitations of it.

The law of detachment can be applied in your life on a variety of levels, but the premise in its purpose is the same. It is essentially, letting go of something or someone to have it or to be closer to them if that is what's meant to be. Equally, it can be the letting go of something or someone to minimize or eliminate heartache, pain or stress. On another level, it is choosing to be in this world, but not of it; by choosing not to participate in the form of attachment. You are choosing to be untethered, by not attaching yourself to any person, place or thing.

You will still interact with people, go places and acquire things, but your life will not be dependent on the very same people, places or things. This way of living is freedom. Freedom to love and be loved. The freedom to travel to your heart's content. Freedom to have your hearts desires and the freedom to go on should you not.

Sometimes we find that in order to maintain a certain level of connection to someone or something, you have to keep them or it at a distance. There is freedom afforded to you in this detachment. It allows you to find the calm in your chaos. This calm comes from the peace of mind, heart, and soul that is a by-product of detachment. With detachment, you should have nothing pulling at your heart-strings.

Detaching doesn't mean you sever the connection. Instead, it's more like surrendering to your situation in the moment, by letting go, to get the outcome that you desire to have. So that by not attaching yourself to anything, you free yourself to receive everything.

Let's take relationships for instance; you have a rocky relationship with someone who you love dearly, but you just cannot seem to see eye to eye. You can't get along no matter how hard you try. You have your ups together sure, but the downs make you question whether the ups are worth it. Now imagine, you haven't seen each other in a while.

Time has gone by; you haven't even spoken to this person until something brings you two together again, and at that moment you can think of nothing else except that you are happy to see each other. You realize how much you miss each other and you're reminded of the love that you have for one another. You recognize that being away from each other has somehow bought you closer to each other. Distance made the heart grow fonder. Did it not? What you did was to hold on to one another by letting each other go. It was vital to the relationship but also vital to your sanity and the freedom from stress.

- ❖ **Are you a controlling person or are you more likely to be controlled by others?**
- ❖ **Do you find yourself imposing on the lives of others in any form or fashion?**
- ❖ **Are you allowing others to impose on your life in any form or fashion?**

In answering the above questions in detail, you should be able to ascertain any attachments and *why*? It is in knowing the "why," that should enable you to see the importance as well as the benefit of pulling back and allowing others to live their lives; by recognizing the effects that attachments have in and on our lives. In the same way, it should help you to understand how beneficial it can be for you to set boundaries by pulling back or detaching yourself from the controlling reigns of others, giving you the freedom to live your life.

You remember I mentioned that once upon a time I would not make a move without first consulting with my near and dears. Until I'd finally reached a point in my life where I began to recognize my dependence for what it was, and I started to seek my freedom. In particular, my dependency on my then, closest friend, put her into a position of authority over my life. I empowered her and gave her permission to do this by continually depending on her to tell me what to do because I trusted her thoughts, opinions, and way of life over my own. However, in doing that, I also gave up my freedom to just be me; flaws and all. I was hindering my growth as a human being.

There came a time when I found myself at a point of desiring to live my life as an independent; an individual, but I needed to break the pattern that I'd built over time by my dependency. I was also afraid of letting go and falling flat on my face because I'd had someone else making significant decisions about my life for so long, that I was unsure if I'd be able to handle my own life!

Essentially, I was pretending at living life . . . So to speak. Pretending because had I been "in charge," I would have done certain things differently. Don't get me wrong; I made decisions on my own. I took actions, spoke words and did deeds of my own volition, but still, I did a lot of consulting. Therefore, I was pretending that my life was something it wasn't and it wasn't serving me well.

Going through that situation helped me to realize a lot about myself, my friend and life in general. After all, who are you if you have no control over your life? If someone else is making the majority of your decisions for you as if you were a child, what is your purpose, other than carrying out the will of others, if you're not the decision maker of your life? As children we need it, but as adults, we have the ability to be the authority over our lives. Seeking guidance from the more knowledgeable and wise is a smart move. Not being able to freely live your life because you have to consult about it, get permission for it or are needing to be assured about your *every* move, is not. It's unhealthy because you are creating a scenario of dependency.

This is where learning how to let go frees you. You'd be surrendering to the unknown. Choosing not to limit yourself, allowing yourself to be limited or attempting to restrict others when we set our sights on one outcome or what we believe the result should be. Just as we want for ourselves, we are allowing the people in our lives to live as they are; choosing not to judge the people or their situations. I recognize that this isn't always easy to do because we are a "detail-oriented" species. Meaning, we have to be in the know. Which makes surrendering to the unknown a little harder for some, but having faith in uncertainty indeed is the path to freedom.

Learning to let go, to surrender or to detach, is worth knowing how to do because you give yourself a degree of freedom that is otherwise unattainable. Sure, you can know of, identify with and experience a *type* of freedom, but none of it will be like this; because this is more like the freedom of *being* free.

- **Not forcing others to make a move**
- **Not forcing others to heal or seek help to live better**
- **Not forcing others to choose a path or a direction in which to flow**
- **Stepping back and allowing your loved ones to learn their life lessons just as you have**
- **Accepting people where they are and situations for what they are**

We can't make people want to do better. We shouldn't try to change the lives of others uninvited. Instead, be the example; it speaks louder. Sitting by watching and remaining uninvolved isn't the easiest of things to do for some of us, but in doing this, you free yourself and keep yourself free to be there for those who *are* seeking your support. Refrain from imposing on the life of another. Never take for granted, the importance of being in the position of helping others. Never support from a "God-like" point of view. We're all living this human experience; none of who, are above the other.

If you do a little reflecting, you'll remember that anything that you've ever truly wanted for yourself and you were willing to do the work for, you got, or you're on your way to receiving! The same goes for the loved ones in and around your life. Your needs and wants are right within your grasp! Just remember that when you want to hold on to something, you let it go. The sooner you let it go, the sooner you will have it.

CHAPTER 8

The Power of Power

You were created in greatness, from greatness, and with greatness. Why aren't you living as the powerful, magnificent being that you truly are? It's because you don't yet know who and what you really are!

I don't think we realize just how much power we give away daily. It wasn't until I started paying attention to it that I realized just how much that was for me. Simple things that we don't even think anything of. Allowing others to have power over you by being passive, submissive, overly accepting, overly apologetic; the list goes on. Without even giving it a second thought, we unconsciously allow others to exert their power over us.

If the thought of, the presence of, or the actions of another person can evoke some form of emotional response from you, that you cannot control, they have power over you. So this power, what is it? Power, by the very definition of the word and its implied meaning to this particular chapter, is

"the capacity or ability to direct or influence the behavior of others or the course of events." (Online reference – Oxford Dictionaries)

Now, keeping that very definition in mind and referencing it, as needed, I want you to apply that "power" to yourself at this moment if you don't already hold this belief about your abilities for yourself. This is the quintessential detail of this entire book. YOU HOLD THE POWER!"

Let me start with a scenario that I know will push against the beliefs of many and that's ok because unapologetically, it is *my* truth and falls in line with *my* beliefs, views, and ideas. I think it's important to have an open mind about the beliefs held by others, as it broadens your exposure to the outlook on, of and about life, from the hearts, minds, and eyes of others; thereby offering you a broader perspective on your own beliefs and outlook on life as well. So I say to you, don't close your mind to the possibilities; and on an added note, don't underestimate the power of questioning.

I have learned, and it has worked well for me, to question my responses with "why." For example:

Why did I react this way?
Why does it make me feel this way?
Why do I believe this way?
Why do I feel so strongly about this or that?

I question everything with "why" until the answer is at its most basic. I call this the "heart" of things. You see, it's because of using this method for myself, that I believe you can better understand your beliefs by being able to answer the "why" to your responses and reactions to things, thus enabling you to stand firmly in said beliefs.

While I believe that there is a power, a source if you will, that governs this universal order, I do not believe in a God outside of myself for living *this* life. Let me help you to understand what I mean. We are taught and it is written, in the bible, a book that most of us have read and a great many of who believe in it, that we were created in "His" image. "Him" being God for clarification and descriptive purposes. We believe our "God" to be omnipresent. We believe that "He" is all knowing. We believe that He has the power to perform miracles at will. We believe that He lives in all of us. We believe that He is a "he." Am I on the right path so far? Only you can decide this for yourself. So I'll lay out a little history, according to the books, first. As a side note, let me also say that I am a **firm** believer in getting the **whole** picture when someone quotes something to me. So, seeing as how it is not my intent to insert by way of quoting, the entire Bible into this book, I encourage you to read each quoted section in its entirety.

The following scriptures are quoted from The Holy Bible, New Century Version®, copyright © 1987, 1988, 1991 by Word Publishing, a division of Thomas Nelson, Inc. Used by permission.

Genesis 1:26-27

*26: Then God said, "Let **us** make human beings in **our images and likeness**. And let them rule over the fish in the sea and the birds in the sky, over the tame animals, over all the earth, and over all the small crawling animals on the earth."*

*27: So God created human beings in his image. **In the image of God** he created them. He created them male and female.*

Genesis 2:8-9, 15-16, 21-23

8: Then the Lord God planted a garden in the east, in a place called Eden, and put the man he had formed into it.

9: The Lord God caused every beautiful tree and every tree that was good for food to grow out of the ground. In the middle of the garden, God put the tree that gives life and also the tree that gives the knowledge of good and evil.

15: The Lord God put the man in the Garden of Eden to care for it and work it.

16: The Lord God commanded him, "You may eat the fruit from any tree in the garden,

17: but you must not eat the fruit from the tree which gives the knowledge of good and evil. If you ever eat fruit from that tree, you will die!"

21: So the Lord God caused the man to sleep very deeply, and while he was asleep, God removed one of the man's ribs. Then God closed up the man's skin at the place where he took the rib.

22: The Lord God used the rib from the man to make the woman, and then he brought the woman to the man.

23: And the man said, "Now, this is someone whose bones came from my bones, whose body came from my body. I will call her 'woman,' because she was taken out of man."

Genesis 3:22

*22: Then the Lord God said, "**The man has become <u>like one of us</u>**; he knows good and evil. We must keep him from eating some of the fruit from the tree of life, or he will live forever."*

If you were to keep reading and you have belief in what the bible says, then from my interpretation of verse 24, there exists a place on the face of *this* earth, where we will find a tree of life, guarded in some capacity (natural or supernatural) from which, if eaten from, we will live forever. Do your research. Question everything!

Now, here is why I do not believe in a God outside of myself. When I first read this book for true understanding, that's when I began to see things from a different point of view. Prior to the point of seeking *true* understanding about *my* life, I'd read this book over and over throughout the years and never caught on to some of the things I began to notice once I decided to approach that understanding from a different point of view.

I didn't come to the idea of this approach on my own. In fact, someone made a comment that was so plain and simple, yet powerfully impactful and full of sense, that when I heard the words come out of her mouth, the light bulb went off and I heard a mental bell ringing "ding, ding, ding,' *this* was the answer, specific to me, that I was seeking. I didn't even know that I was seeking that answer until I heard the words.

So Velecia, I thank you for inviting me into your home and taking the time to sit and chat with me. I remember you telling me that I was on your heart and mind and that you didn't know why, but you *felt* like you were supposed to have a conversation with me along the lines of the train of thought from which you spoke. Everything you said to me was essential to my understanding and my life at that moment point; and I absorbed it, but the most profound thing you said to me, was to "take it literally." That statement was so impactful and said in passing so casually. It single-handedly changed my perspective right at that moment. You said, "I don't know why people don't just take the bible literally."

A door opened for me with those words. Not as if I hadn't had thoughts or ideas about things that went against popular belief; but those words gave me a confirmation, of sorts that, it was *ok* to explore and delve deeper into something that I'd previously been conditioned not to believe in and to reject.

As if thinking of, exploring, studying about or even believing in something other than the popular belief would be violating some law; earth-tied or universal.

Well, if I'm to take what I've read in the above-quoted scriptures literally, then at the top of my list of questions is, 'Who is "us"?' Under popular belief, there is only one God. Under popular belief, there is none like Him, and also popular belief, God created the heavens and the earth alone?

John 1:1-4

1: *In the beginning there was the Word. The Word was with God, and the Word was God.*

2: *He was with God in the beginning.*

3: *All things were made by him, and nothing was made without him.*

4: *In him there was life, and that life was the light of all people.*

My interpretation: He is one. So again, who is "us"?

According to what we've learned about our creation, we were made in his image *and* likeness. So unless you believe that the writer was using two different words to describe the same thing, it's feasible to perceive that the writer is describing two parts of a whole. Therefore, his image and his likeness, taken literally, would mean how he *looks* and how he *is*; referring to his capabilities. Since he created us in his image and likeness, it is my assumption that not only do we look like him, but we come also equipped, with the same abilities and capabilities as him. He essentially created mini versions of himself.

With this assumed visual of image and likeness, I've deduced that during the creation of human beings, Adam, at his inception, was but a shell. His eyes were wide open, but still, he was not awake. Having some knowledge and understanding, but only to a degree. He had the *capacity* to know all that his creator knew but was not "*allowed*" to know. Incidentally, it was ok for Adam to live on forever, just as his God; and he could be like his God in this way because the tree of life wasn't forbidden to him, only the tree of knowledge of good and evil.

My interpretation: This was a form of control.

With an assumed capacity of human capabilities based on the description given about everything created on earth (Genesis 1:26) and the power of dominion of said creations given to humans by God, we are capable of being the authority over ourselves and everything, created by God, that lives on and inhabits this earth.

My interpretation: An appeasement; possibly meant to keep humans occupied, lest they start to tap into their dormant capabilities, thus far untapped, because we have not been taught, how to tap into our inherent, god-like gifts, we were equipped with during our creation.

Makes me wonder what life would be like had Adam and Eve chosen to eat from the tree of life first, before partaking in the fruit from the tree of knowledge of good and evil. Interesting food for thought.

So, in light of the above-stated points of view, I do not believe in a God outside of myself because we were created by Him, in His image and likeness, with a piece of him in all of us. We're given power over everything on this earth, including ourselves. I don't mean to take away from or disregard the faith of believers in the power of prayers answered by God. However, for all of the prayers that are sent "out" to God, at the end of the day, the results of those prayers always end up coming to you by way of actions that *you* took, and of which other *people* may have played a part in helping you to manifest. Have you ever thought of it from that viewpoint?

Equally important to me is my belief that we are all energy. Bits and pieces of the whole. Imagine God as a big ball of energy. We are created by him as smaller bursts of energy and together, collectively, we form the whole. So you see, from my perspective, there is no God outside of ourselves because individually, we are parts of God and together we are God. John 1:1

Food For Thought: Awakening Your Power

Has God placed us here on a drop and leave? Left to our own devices to figure this life out; as if on assignment? Whereby, he doesn't interfere with our lives because of free will. Which means every single moment, event and happening in our lives are all created by us; ourselves. No one, nor entity performed any miracles on our behalf. No one, nor entity decided who would and would not be successful in this life; or who would or wouldn't have high or low volumes of material possessions and gains, greater or lesser knowledge, more or less potential.

We were all given equal abilities, coming from the one source, of whose likeness we were created. Therefore, we have the ability to create any life we desire to have. All of us were born with the aptitude for a skill of which we specialize in that aids in allowing us to be individuals. We are all able to bring something different to the table, while still being able to contribute, collectively, to the whole. We come lacking or forgetting this knowledge, but with an equal opportunity to gain or tap into said knowledge. The knowledge of these abilities and what we could be capable of once we tap into them empowers us to live whatever life we so choose. You can't properly steer the wheel if you don't believe you know how to drive. Even now, I am on the journey, seeking a greater understanding of how to tap into this knowledge, these abilities.

Tapping Into Your Greatness: Wielding Your Power

Further along in the book, in chapter 16, we're going to address time and our perception of it, in depth, but I'm going to touch on it just a bit in this chapter, as it pertains to tapping into and wielding your power.

First of all, I believe that time is just a construct meant to control the masses. I delve into it more in-depth in chapter 16, but I'll tell you this; the moment you learn and accept this, the easier it will become to make sense of the multi-directional bits of information that we receive every day, but disregard because it doesn't fall in line with what we believe we know. So for the sake of your understanding, I am speaking in time terms, but I do not believe that time, as we know it, truly exists.

Utilizing your power will involve learning how to bend time to your will; to your control. Not specifically for personal gain, but you will benefit from it. Rather, you need to learn to bend time to control better the direction that you take your life. You will learn to steer the wheel of time in order, to direct your life in the direction you *choose* for it to go. This too may push against your personal beliefs, but it would do you well to take heed open-mindedly.

I give you these instructions and tell you to take heed on whose authority? My own. It doesn't matter, nor should it bother you, that I didn't need to go to school for years on end, spending unnecessary money and racking up unnecessary debt, just to earn a piece of paper that gives me the authority, to a degree, by way of others, to speak on what I *believe* to be true. Taking nothing away from all of the folks who spent all of that valuable time, doing all of that hard work, to earn the degrees that gives them the authority, credibility and financial compensation I might add, on which to stand. I applaud them, sincerely.

However, in tapping into and wielding my power, I operate on my authority, because ultimately it's the only authority that I need. Yes, we must operate in cooperation with the rules and laws not just of this land, but of this world; but that's where the Law of Detachment allows us to continue to move more fluidly within the confines of this world.

I consider myself to be a rebel of sorts, and perhaps my cause is self-serving. Self and soul preservation with absolute awareness is, after all, *my* goal. However, I choose not to hoard this knowledge to myself selfishly. Accumulating knowledge and using it to stay *above* others is power, in the form of control. You see, I believe that knowledge, fully understood, is power; and I aim to share the wealth with anyone who's seeking it. Looking at what you know and believe to be history, and even at this point in our timeline, power has been and is being abused by some, who have more knowledge and resources, and choose to wield the power of having these, to control others.

Power is most beneficial for the whole when used *for* the greater good. Power reaches its highest potential when all sources of it are pulled together, operating as a singularity, one whole. The only reason some of you *believe* you are at the mercy of those who *seem* to be more "powerful" than you are, is because you have not recognized, accepted and risen to the power within you, to be all and anything or anyone that you choose to be.

We are powerful gods in our own right! Not to be confused with being GOD; even if we don't fully comprehend this. But we are nothing compared to the entity we become when we all pull together as one. **That's** a force to be reckoned with! A force that *will* illuminate across time and space because whether we understand or believe it, we *are* headed in this direction. Make no mistake about it.

We come to this earth embedded with a feeling of importance in our genetic make-up. If you have yet to recognize it and are instead going through life with a "need" to feel important, this could mean that you're missing something inside that hasn't allowed you to tap into the greatness that you were born with; and by missing, I mean not seeing or *feeling*. "It's" there, just unrecognized as of yet. You **are** important. Let's get that part straight.

If you find yourself longing for something or desiring a way of life not yet achieved, it's because you *know* there's more to you than meets the eye, but you have yet to learn to tap into that powerful part of you. Either way, **YOU ARE IMPORTANT**! It is only to yourself that you have to prove this to, by way of understanding, believing and accepting this fact; no one else. There's no need for validation. Recognizing your importance aids you in tapping into your power. A person who feels unimportant feels powerless, but a person who knows their importance recognizes and acknowledges that they indeed have power.

Our beliefs are the foundation of which our realities are built. It shapes what we consider to be our "real world." This shaping is due to our perception and how we perceive and process our beliefs. So the processing of our beliefs according to our understanding gives us what results into what we call our reality. This is power.

This is important to understand because it implies that, if and when the way we perceive our beliefs change, so does our reality. This is where the "we are in control of our reality or lives" factor, comes into play. Now to me, that gives me the impression that I can cultivate my reality to be whatever I would like for it to be, based on how I see and process things within and around my life. I can do this because it's all about how I choose to process my world around me in relation to what I believe in; giving me control over my life on a level of my own making. That's power!

Do yourself a favor and eliminate any pessimism in your life. Don't be a pessimist. In fact, there's no room in the life of a powerful decision maker, for pessimism. Don't worry about if and how long it will take to catch on.

The intent and purposeful practice of recognizing your importance and utilizing your power will come with ease, before and without you even knowing it. You are only charged with doing your part of putting it into action.

It's like learning to ride a bike without trainers or another hand to help keep you steady. You need guidance at first until you get the hang of it; but with practice, you're able to take the wheel and steer it on your own, without even thinking about it. Balancing yourself on the wheels, while at the same time, enjoying the breeze from the ride and the sights that you encounter while on your trip.

Tell *your* truth. It's always the best starting point. This is the power of power. Own it!

CHAPTER 9

The Art of Creative Talk-Speak: Being Mindful of How You Talk

Our talk-speak shapes our reality. These are the words that we utter on an everyday basis that flow out of our mouths, using a vocabulary base instilled in us from the time of birth. Without too much conscious effort or thought, when speaking, we are autonomously using our words as an automatic response based on our beliefs and *what* we believe we know. While there are some who understand all too well, the power contained in the tongue we use to convey our thoughts and feelings, by way of our talk-speak, there is also an even greater portion of the earth's population that know nothing of this power, let alone how to use it. Even worse, they have knowledge *and* understanding of this power but *choose* not to use it.

All too often, we are unintentionally abusing a power that's been unknowingly in use since before the time we learned to speak. Mind over matter. How many times have you heard that? How many times have you dismissed that very thought or statement because of a lack of understanding of *how* to wield your mind over matter? How many times have you combined the power of the tongue with your ability to control matter with your mind? Today you're going to read about some ways to make better use of this power.

Proverbs 18:21 KJV

"Death and life are in the power of the tongue: and they that love it shall eat the fruit thereof."

There you have it. Straight from a book that a great many human beings live their lives according to; and yet still, the recognition of a God-given power is overlooked daily and dismissed as just another metaphor. We've all heard this one at some moment point in our lives on the by and by. We've all heard someone say it, have had it told to us or may have even spoken the words to someone ourselves. What you see, however, when taken literally, is a clear description of a power that every human being on the face of this earth has; because we're all born with a tongue. We all learn to communicate using words, no matter the method of delivery. We all have a "talk-speak."

Still, here are some other examples of the power of the tongue described and instructions given on *how* to use it.

1 Peter 3:10

For he that will love life, and see good days, let him refrain his tongue from evil, and his lips that they speak no guile:

Proverbs 15:1

A soft answer turneth away wrath: but grievous words stir up anger.

Ephesians 4:29

Let no corrupt communication proceed out of your mouth, but that which is good to the use of edifying, that it may minister grace unto the hearers.

Matthew 12:36-37

But I say unto you, that every idle word that men shall speak, they shall give account thereof in the day of judgment.

Psalms 141:3

Set a watch, O LORD, before my mouth; keep the door of my lips.

James 3:8

But the tongue can no man tame; [it is] an unruly evil, full of deadly poison.

James 1:26

If any man among you seem to be religious, and bridleth not his tongue, but deceiveth his own heart, this man's religion [is] vain.

Proverbs 10:19

In the multitude of words there wanteth not sin: but he that refraineth his lips [is] wise.

Proverbs 15:28

The heart of the righteous studieth to answer: but the mouth of the wicked poureth out evil things.

James 3:6

And the tongue [is] a fire, a world of iniquity: so is the tongue among our members, that it defileth the whole body, and setteth on fire the course of nature; and it is set on fire of hell.

Proverbs 12:18

There is that speaketh like the piercings of a sword: but the tongue of the wise [is] health.

Proverbs 15:4

A wholesome tongue [is] a tree of life: but perverseness therein [is] a breach in the spirit.

Psalms 19:14

Let the words of my mouth, and the meditation of my heart, be acceptable in thy sight, O LORD, my strength, and my redeemer.

Philippians 2:14

Do all things without murmurings and disputings:

Proverbs 13:3

He that keepeth his mouth keepeth his life: [but] he that openeth wide his lips shall have destruction.

*https://www.kingjamesbibleonline.org/Bible-Verses-About-Power-Of-The-Tongue/

There *is* power in your words. A force that is drawn from you and your belief in those words when you speak them. Why do you think people give so much merit to the adage of being careful of what you say? Still, they only understand that there's some truth to the statement, but they don't fully understand the real power of the tongue, even as they speak. Somewhere within them, they believe that speaking words can make things happen. Repeating a word of caution, when they see fit, by force of habit because they've heard the saying at some point in their lives. It resonated with them, and instinctively they share it when someone says something that prompts them to speak those words of warning or advice if you will.

All the while, never giving real thought to what it is they're actually saying or why they're even saying it. Disregarding the belief, whether consciously or subconsciously, that a person *can* speak things into existence. Knowingly or unknowingly, no matter the scale on which it was learned, the saying is now embedded in the subconscious, and it is spoken, upon provocation, because it is believed to be true.

Growing up and throughout my young adulthood, I'd heard on many occasions, among other adages, that we should never lie about the death of a living person, nor should we lie about something being wrong with your vehicle. You hear these sayings coming from the mouths of others; mostly your elders with more experience living this life than you, thus far. Words of advice and warnings to take heed to, but for lack of understanding the real power, they actually held.

Some years ago in my early thirties, I purchased a vehicle, a minivan old and worn; but at the time, it was all that I could afford so that I would have some type of vehicle for transportation for me and my girls. I was a single mom at that point. I'd just left my husband of six years who'd been in my life only two years before our getting married. I was working a full-time job doing my best to manage and balance work, house, and home. I'd had plenty of moments where I didn't feel up to going into work. Most times, with no choice but to go in if we were to have some sort of income; but there were times when giving in to the feeling of not wanting to be bothered, I'd call in, making up one excuse or another as to why I wouldn't be able to make it in for the day.

Then came the time where I would gain a full understanding of the reality of speaking things into existence and why you should never speak words that you know aren't true. I called into work one day because my "van wouldn't start" for me. Umm hmm . . . I made it up. Had a whole story to go with it too. I'd carefully thought of my words and then carefully constructed them in a way that would give me the favorable result I desired, which in this case was permission to be out of work without penalty.

We don't realize, that when we're constructing a lie within our minds, that we are visualizing it, *feeling* it and then articulating it in such a way as to be *believable* — thereby creating a directive, to the universe, to God or the God within, whichever your preference. Either way, you have set into motion a sequence of events to be brought into fruition by the manifestation of said events through the utterance of your words.

Well, there came the point and much too quickly I might add, where the van decided that it could go no further. Not too long after I'd called out for the very same reason, my van just stopped one day and would not come on. It was old and worn, but it had worked well for me up until that point, of which it just conked out on me with no warning whatsoever that it was going to do so. It was on that day that I gained a full understanding of why you should never lie about your vehicle, but even more significant than that, just how powerful our thoughts and words could be.

Here it is, about ten years later, and I have only just begun in the past few years to learn to start focusing on that prevailing notion that I'd discovered earlier on in my life. It's becoming more of an accepted idea amongst us humans, as we evolve and gain a deeper understanding of this concept. What I'm trying to impart onto you, is the notion that it's more than just a theory. Your talk-speak is power!

Learning to talk in such a way that you are mindful of your words at any given time, is indeed a skill. By mastering this skill, the world that you can create for yourself is damn near limitless. Seriously! Impossible is a pessimistic word that can only be meant to put restrictions on what you believe you can and cannot do. What you believe you can and cannot be. However, in mastering this skill, you will learn that *nothing* is impossible; only what you believe to be.

This skill takes a lot of practice. It doesn't come to you overnight. Nor does the mindset that you'll need to hone in on this concept. You'll have to press on in spite of the challenges it'll bring that will go against your current beliefs. What you believe to be the way of life and truth. Changing your mindset takes a string of moment points and the happenings within them, to bring it about, but it *is* possible; and before you know it, you'll be thinking and talking in such a way, that it'll be hard to believe that *you* once believed and spoke any other way before that point.

You are a divine creation. What you think about, talk about, accept and expect *will* manifest. This is why it's so vital for you to adjust your mindset to that of a mind that will, no matter the challenges it may face, always find the positivity to focus on, think on and speak on. Thus, manifesting a string of positive moments in your life, while you're here on this earth.

This will not only enhance the quality of your life, but it will also serve to improve the quality of the lives around you. You'll need to trust your divinity. Own it! Wielding this power cannot be done if you don't believe it to be true. If this is your state of mind at this moment, then do your research! Take the information received that piqued your interest or stood out to you, or even that you challenge, and start by doing your research to come to a better understanding of where you stand in your beliefs regarding who you indeed are.

You have to know and believe that you are created to be just like the Source; and that you *are* connected to the Source. We've been given information that tells us so. No matter the religion, the land or the language, as the stories go, there is a Source of some sort, a Creator if you will, who created the humankind and did so in its image. All that I am asking you to do is to trust yourself, who and what you are, and the powers that are within you. You have been armed with the knowledge that empowers you to rewrite your agreement with *this* reality. It's up to you to actually use it.

Use your words, charged by your thoughts, to alter the direction of your life. It doesn't matter how old you are, where you are in life, what resources you have or lack. If you can wrap your head around what's being told to you and learn to start implementing these teachings into your life, *none* of the above stated will matter anymore because your life *will* change, naturally.

Be mindful of how you think, act and speak. How you treat yourself and others; how you use what you learn. Use your God-given, inherently miraculous, gift and get creative with it. Taking care not to be selfish with it or you'll risk self-sabotage. Learn to be more mindful of what it is you *truly* want, unless you want to find yourself repeatedly learning the lesson, of being careful of what you ask for. Most importantly, be responsible with it. It is, after all, a power.

CHAPTER 10

Change & Adaptability: Are You Adaptable?

Here is an inevitable fact of life: change is constant. During this lifetime, you'll experience the type of change of which you can control, and then there'll be the type of change of which you'll have little to no control. In knowing this to be fact, we also understand and accept that change will affect us invariably. To deal with and better operate in the moment to moment points of our lives, we've all found ourselves, at some point or another, having to make or adapt to some form of change.

Some of us have also had to learn, the hard way, that accepting and adapting to change isn't always so easy to do, yet it is inevitable. Ultimately, being adaptable and learning to use your power of will can help you through any change. Whether that change is initiated by you or enters your life from unforeseeable circumstances, you are empowered with choice when you know how to adapt.

For the sake of clear understanding of the meaning of and the difference between the two, here are the definitions to change and adaptable, according to the Oxford Dictionaries which can be found online at https://www.oxforddictionaries.com

> *Change*
> *Verb •   1.make or become different: "a proposal to change the law."*
> - *2.take or use another instead of: "she decided to change her name."*

Noun
- 1. the act or instance of making or becoming different: *"the change from a nomadic to an agricultural society."*

- 2. coins as opposed to paper currency: *"a handful of loose change."*

Adaptable
Adjective • 1. able to adjust to new conditions: *"rats are highly adaptable to change."*

My experience has been, that in all things, anytime you go against the natural flow of what you know, there's always opposition. You create struggle, hardships and unnecessary heartache and pain for yourself; only to find yourself inevitably stepping in line with the flow of things anyway. Consequently, you're just delaying the inevitable.

Sometimes it's hard to recognize when we are creating strife in our lives. Strife that's hard to recognize because it can appear under the guise of "going against the grain, acting or being different." Please don't get me wrong. I'm by no means saying that we should block our creative ideas and notions just to play it safe. I am saying though, that perhaps you should try, as best you can, to make sure that you have solid footing; or at the very least, you're setting yourself up to step out on a firm foundation. This applies to you even when you are stepping out on faith into the unknown. It won't eliminate all of the lessons you'll learn along the way. (I use lesson(s) in place of failure(s) that you may experience) However, you should be able to minimize them.

I've heard it said on many occasions, the definition of insanity was doing the same thing over and over again, each time expecting a different result. Honey let me tell you, according to this line of belief, I've been walking around crazy, deranged and insane for the majority of my life! It took me a long time (emphasis on LONG) to get to the point of applying this concept to my life. I needed to accept that this was true and that it was *my* truth. I had to come to a point where I not only believed in this statement but of also recognizing, understanding and accepting that I was actually doing what the statement implied! I was living a life of self-imposed hardship, created by self-sabotage and voluntary insanity.

I hated to admit it for a very long time, but I was not a person who did well with change. Let *me* tell the story though, and I was one who flowed with and like the wind. To a degree, I was what I termed myself as, a 'wind flow-er'; in that I could easily make changes that most other people I knew in my life, were not only unwilling to make, but frowned upon, because *my* changes spoke to my stability or instability as it were, and my ability to *remain* stable.

For the better part of my adult life, from the time I got into the very first apartment of my own, I've been changing addresses like there was no tomorrow. A lot of my moves were because I wasn't responsible with my finances, but even that was because I lacked discipline. As far as I was concerned, anything that I had to be "disciplined" for, was *something* trying to have authority over me; and let me tell you, I rebelled any authoritative figure or entity seeking to govern my being. Period!

I called myself trying to be in control of my life by doing what I had to do any time I found myself in an adverse situation. When in truth, I was out of control. I kept putting myself into those "adverse situations." The very lack of discipline and my inability to yield to any authority was propelling me in a spiraled, downward, never-ending, stairwell of chaos. This chaos had become my norm, and I couldn't even recognize it as such, because I was too deep in it and ill-equipped I might add, to be able to recognize and accept it for what it was.

I would eventually get to the place of gaining an understanding of the benefits of having discipline and self-control in my life that helped me to see that being adaptable made me flexible and versatile. It gave me flexibility and increased my versatility. Therefore, I was still able to flow with the wind; just more responsibly.

It was when I started to open to the acceptance of change that my ability to adapt began to hone in. This acceptance only happened when I finally said, 'Enough is enough. Something has to give.' And not just say it, but I had to reach the point in my life when I *felt* that statement just as strongly as I *meant* it when I spoke it. Aside from the birth of my children, my life had no definition. I never finished anything I started; even though I was always good at anything, I did. I had nothing to show for my years on this earth, except my children. I just woke up one day and decided that enough was enough.

Looking back on it, I can see some of the moment points in my life where I was being nudged to start accepting and implementing discipline in my life. Opportunities were arising here and there, to gain insight from a different perspective. I even remember, clear as day, when I put my foot down and said, 'this is it. I can't keep repelling discipline and authority in my life. I need discipline in my life, and this is how I'm going to get it.' Then, in that very moment, I stood up during the altar call and walked to the altar in the church that I'd been visiting for a while, and I joined it.

In that moment point of my life, the church offered discipline and authority from a higher power that governed over my life as was my belief at that time. It was the perfect place and opportunity for me to begin submitting to a will other than my own. Giving me some much-needed structure to my life; in addition to the discipline and authority. The lessons that I would learn and take with me when my time came to depart and separate from the church are too numerous to name. However, I can tell you that my life is definitely the better for it and I wouldn't change anything about my time there, given the opportunity.

Before switching gears, let me just note that, what I've deduced from my experiences during this string of moment points that is my life, is that being more willing to adapt to any change based on new knowledge, information or circumstances that you readily accept and believe, can have an overwhelmingly positive effect on your life. Opening doors unseen but very necessary for you to move on to new levels of your life.

This is as opposed to the hardships one can encounter from the rejection of any new knowledge, information or circumstances and the unwillingness to adapt to the inevitable change the above mentioned represents.

Tapping into our inner senses cannot be willed. You have to reach a certain level of understanding first. Not only do our egos lack any control where our inner senses are concerned, but our ego must also be sat down, laid to rest and put into the position of second, so to speak. We do this so that our inner senses can move freely and without restriction imposed upon us from our egos need, to control everything. The ego is an extension of your body and earth essence; the personality we come into upon our arrival into this world. In truth, it is the soul that should rule the body and not the body or ego controlling the soul.

The progression of the evolution into our higher selves and the ability to tap into and use our inner senses is dependent on our ability to control the suppression of our egos. Control is necessary because it will involve a lot of change and dependency on our ability to adapt and your ego will fight you along the way because your evolution consists of the ego's relinquishing of control.

One of the purposes that our ego serves is that, of keeping us actively informed in our conscious wake. Delivering processed information, obtained from the subconscious that we would otherwise forget; even though our actions are a reflection of and in response to said information from the subconscious. We are not eliminating our egos. Our egos are a big part of our personalities. Instead, we are teaching the ego to work in harmony and submission to, our higher selves. The god within.

Our egos operate using the outer senses while our higher selves or entities operate using the inner senses. These inner senses are the inherent gifts we gain during our creation. Conversely, the ego impedes the awareness and abilities of the subconscious on a conscious level. Yet, the ego is necessary if we are to have conscious awareness of subconscious communication. It's like a paradox almost.

We don't control things in this world the way we *think* we do. We're so busy trying to be the sole controlling authority over our "selves," that we are blocking any real access to the *knowing* of who and what we truly are in our natural form and the abilities of which we are capable. We are not these bodies that we inhabit; we are so much more!

We can't adapt to anything we're not open to receiving. Change is going to happen, whether it's accepted or not; and while we do have control over some of the change that occurs throughout our lives, I want you to keep in mind that the change I speak of is any change that occurs *outside* of our control.

It is vital to our growth that we position ourselves to be able to adapt to change in order to better move about in this life. It enables an inner-growth that will allow for a more significant life experience with our outer senses. A more significant life experience, stemming from internal growth, becomes a life made from the substance of high quality.

To do this, I believe we have to surrender. This decision that you've made will be a multi-faceted success. It will be dependent on many parts contributing to the whole. The ultimate end-result that you are aiming to achieve cannot be obtained by the changing of one thing or behavior. It will take a combination of contributions, mentally, physically and from that of your consciousness; spiritually if you will.

Understanding how your inner and outer senses play a part in your ability to accept and adapt to change will only aid in your journey to successfully completing whatever it is that you aim to achieve from it all.

You are wielding two sets of power. One of which you think has more pull because you are aware of it. You may not even recognize it as a power, but it might do you well to start thinking of it and treating it as what it is. You're *aware* of your conscious thought and actions. The power in this is that you're able to use your outer senses to control your actions which are based on your conscious thought.

As for your inner senses, that power tends to lie dormant for lack of awareness, but they're still a power you possess of which, with practice, you'll be able to use to better aid you in controlling your reality. This makes your inner-senses even more potent than that of your outer senses since your outer senses control what's happening *within* your reality. While your inner senses, your subconscious, is controlling your *actual* reality.

Knowing this and understanding what it is precisely that this means; isn't it about time that you surrendered to yourself? If you know and believe that you are indeed consciousness, powerful in your own right, then choose to demote your ego and take away the authority it has held over your entire life on this earth thus far. Allow your consciousness (a combo of both the conscious and subconscious) the free reign it needs to propel you to your next level.

Your ego will become the controlee as opposed to being the controller. A true understanding of this will free you in ways that cannot be defined nor described in the way that we know things to be. However, I believe that as you become a walking example of the inevitable change that this will bring about, without having to say much, once you are freed by your true understanding of things, you will speak to the inner knowing and understanding of others. Allowing you to reach the masses, one consciousness at a time.

We are, after all, a part of one great big consciousness. A collective so to speak. However, we have been operating as a disconnected collective for so long, that some of us have to be reminded of who we really are.

Not wanting to contradict myself, let me place this disclaimer here by saying to you that I do believe that we operate in free will . . . to a degree. Also, I don't think it possible to stray too far from what our ultimate purposes are for being here in *this* lifetime. Therefore ultimately, it's possible that free will is but an illusion.

That being said, I'm going to share with you a journal entry written while on my journey to learning to tap into *my* inner senses. I share this in the hopes of helping you to understand that this journey isn't easy or straightforward by any means. There's so much to learn. So much that we don't know. However, I've learned to approach this with an open mind. A mind opened so immensely that I feel and believe that I'm almost at the point of a clean slate, with all of the knowledge and experience gained thus far, but no convictions that will close me off to any other possibilities.

- *What can I do to change this or the outcome of this situation?*
- *My emotions are trying to get the best of me but how will they aid me at this moment? What kind of actual change will it give or bring to my circumstances?*
- *How can any of my outer senses help me at this moment? Change this moment? Change the outcome of my circumstances?*

I'm really and truly beginning to believe that free will is nothing but an illusion. And if that's true, then my moment points will be my moment points, no matter how random and spontaneous they may seem or that I thought them to be. Which means I can do nothing about it outwardly and very possibly inwardly. Since my higher self, my entity whole, holds all of the cards.

And this means that maybe I should try, for once, instead, to surrender to my moments of seeming chaos. Do I lose power in this way? By doing this? Am I giving up by giving in? Or am I taking control by surrendering my will to a deeper part of me that currently has a knowing and understanding that I do not yet have an understanding of, in my conscious wake?

Do I trust in the things that I speak about? Do I believe it and believe in it? Can I and will I surrender to it? I recognize that something is off. Something is different. For me anyway, my inner eyes have been opened, and I can't turn them off, close them or shut them down. Nor do I want to.

I can't ignore everything that I've learned and come to believe, but I'm now at the moment point in my life where I don't know what to do with the information that I'm learning and have come to believe. I don't know how to use it, but I have the desire to learn. I want to know what to do with it and how to use it effortlessly.

After all is said and done, I choose not to fight it; not to go against it. I'm going to allow my mind to relax by trying not to focus on the micro details. Regulating any distractions that may arise and allow myself to let go. Drop. Release and give in.

Imagine being able to dig deep within and pull out a better, new and improved version of yourself. The possibilities that reveal themselves to you when you start making the necessary change(s) and adapting your life according to are endless. I recognize that for some, even the *thought* of change can be daunting. I myself used to be among those that felt this way. I want to let you know, however, that you are not alone. In anything that you do and every single moment throughout your life, you are never alone. It's not as hard as you may think and it *is* very possible.

Remember to flow with the changes that are happening in and around your life as opposed to trying to fight against them. You'll have more control going with the flow than not. Trying to go against it, could cause you to detrimentally catapult your life into hardships way beyond what you had to endure.

If it is so, that we will inevitably end up having to adapt to some form of change that's affecting our lives anyway; why not take the most natural path to get to that point? Work smart, not hard. Smart not hard. Smart not hard. You get the picture.

Chapter 11

The Path Less Traveled

Prepare yourself

For the road you are about to travel on has only been visited by few

Each with his own directive and the outcome, no one knew

Though the other path seemed easier and more within our ability to withstand

The prospect of what was waiting, made less daunting, the unknown that lay ahead

Mecheline Muhammad

As previously mentioned, it has been my experience over the years that, when it seems like nothing will go right for you; when everything seems to be falling apart and every step forward feels like five to ten steps back; those might be signs that things are being forced or held on to when perhaps it's time to let go. I'm talking about circumstances, situations and relationships that are either, not being allowed to progress naturally, or that should no longer be held on to. Only, you won't allow it to be free.

I'm of the mindset that when a person tries to force something that shouldn't be; or hold on to what should probably be let go of, the universe always has a way of balancing the order. Setting the equation right. Always it will be, the way it was supposed to be. No matter the route that's taken. Your denial of this and your desire to hold on tight to what you should let go will only delay what will be, no matter what you do to try and stop or change it.

The path of least resistance is best. Although, not always the easiest nor the desired path. Sometimes, because of lack of foresight and trust, we human beings feel like we can control things that were never actually in our control from the get-go.

It's sad really because we spend our whole lives trying to control and master a life that we may not control at all. I know it seems as though some people live this life better than others. Although it's probably unjust to make such a comparison when people can't help being in or from the families they were born into, or can they?

What I have noticed is that people who own their truth, tend to fare pretty well. Ultimately, we should all be living in our truth. Looking at it for what it is. Accepting that whatever your life is at the moment, it is your truth. Then, owning it! Own your truth! What you don't like about what you see, you can always change. Nothing and I repeat nothing has to remain as is. You can always grow. Your only limitations stem from doubt of self. Remember who you are!

Take away what you don't like and work with what you *do* like about yourself. Start new habits. Increase your knowledge. Do a detox of your circle; the people you keep around you. Take a good look at what you are subconsciously feeding yourself. Build on the parts of you that you are proud of. The parts of you that you actually like. The parts of you that have the potential to take you to where you want to be. All you need to do is be real with yourself!

Here's something that some of you may have to let soak in for a bit. Everyone isn't meant to go with you to the level you are rising. The level you are about to be on. And let me be clear; no matter where you are in life, what's going on in it, and who you currently have or don't have in your life, if you are forward moving and forward thinking, in other words growing; you are bound to find yourself shedding folks in and around your circle.

When you finally decide to change your life for the better, you'll find your share of supporters and haters. Your sabotagers, blockers and "misery loves company" folks. Some of you will also have a strong support team. Family and friends that not only want to see you living life as your best you; but are helping you to do so and working towards coming along with you by bettering themselves as well.

Some are not so fortunate to have such support, but I assure you that's not altogether a bad thing. There are a plethora of benefits to being alone and spending time with yourself. Often times, we'll associate being alone with the meaning of being lonely. When, if used to your benefit, the *act* of being alone, can increase the *quality* of your life and livelihood.

Here is a list of reasons that the act of being alone can be of benefit to you.

Self-Discovery: One of the key objectives of this entire book is the discovery of self. You are learning yourself. Figuring out who you are; and more importantly, <u>what</u> you are. After all, how can you thoroughly enjoy this life and everything it brings forth, when you're not making use of everything it has to offer, without an understanding of who you are?

I mean, we are a far greater and a more complex being of life, than we even know. For a moment, imagine those of us who purchase MacBook's, PCs and Smart Phones. We know the basics of using it. We even take the time to learn how to use *some* of its features; the "advertised" features. However, seeing as how many of them no longer come with user manuals anymore, we never seem to take the time to learn *all* about them. Let alone what they're fully capable of and the benefits of learning about and then using the features of the machines.

We have access to the manuals, but how many of you actually download them or go the website to take the time to read through them? I mean really read through them and try out all of the features of the machine. Learn how to put them to use so that your device is of even better use to you? Do you get where I'm going with this?

The act of being alone gives us the opportunity to discover ourselves without the interference of outside noise. For me, personally, I'm a retreater. Most of the people that I keep close in my life know or have learned that I'm a retreater. If a person in my life doesn't know this about me, they're more than likely, not as close to me as they may think they are. However, those who know that I'm a retreater, also know or have learned not to take it personally.

When I retreat, I pull back from everything and everyone. While I have always been a retreater, it hasn't always been the ideal thing to do. Seeing as how at one time, I was a single mother with four kids and I had responsibilities that I really couldn't afford to stay away from. I found myself suffering the self-inflicted consequences of my retreats. I was pulling away from the world and the noise, trying to reignite my inner flame. Re-energize me. Shed any weight in the form of problems, concerns or issues I may have been carrying at the time; and gaining some sort of peace of mind. Looking for my calm in the midst of my chaos.

Naturally, I didn't have the understanding back then as I do now. I know now that I was never actually solving any problems because I didn't know *how* to use those retreats to their fullest and my benefit. All I ever really accomplished back then was to enclose myself into a bubble that essentially blocked out any of the noise around me. Never actually solving any problems or lifting any weight off of my shoulders; and as I think of it, there was little to any self-actualization.

The end result to those retreats back then was an eventual emergence back into the unresolved chaos that awaited me upon my return into the "real world." I still had the same issues and problems. They were just put on hold until I felt like dealing with them.

In my later years, because of my husband, I've been afforded the opportunity to stay home with my children, and I found myself with a lot of time on my hands. It took me a little while to find a balance, but I've learned to put that time with myself to better use. I was being forced, in a sense, to spend time with myself. Something that I used to dread.

I have a very active mind, and thoughts and ideas are always flowing. Being alone sometimes drove me crazy because I didn't know how to shut down my thoughts. This is why I used to dread being alone. In the presence of other people, I could run my mouth. Still popping off thoughts and ideas, but now I'm able to talk about it, amongst other things, with someone, which helped to get it out of my system.

I choose to retreat now because by doing so, I'm not having to worry about the distraction of speaking to people and I deal only with the noise that I care to. Now I use this time to go within. I try to tap into inner parts of myself that I have yet to reach. Hone in on my truth. Tap into my God-like, birth inherent powers. The getting to know yourself part isn't a one-day event; It's not instantaneous, and it won't happen overnight. It's a constant work in progress that you have to give attention and effort to.

I can still handle my business while on retreat, and I've learned to channel my thoughts through writing to get it out of my head, without having to speak it to someone else. I've always been a writer. I've always kept "journals," books of songs, poems, thoughts, and ideas — all random and in no particular order. However, as I've grown, I've learned to put to better use that skill. I still keep books of all sorts with my writings, but now they're organized. I make better use of them by using them to help me to collect my thoughts and ideas in such a way, that I'm able to create from them, something that can be of use not only to myself but to others as well.

My thoughts on self-discovery? The more you put into practice trying to discover yourself, the more you will learn about yourself. The more you learn about yourself, the more you know. The more you know about yourself, the more you grow. Repeat.

Privacy: Privacy allows you the time and ability to let loose in whatever manner you deem necessary to make better use out of your time alone.

Meditation: I can go on and on about the benefits of meditation. The way it helps you to get in touch with yourself. How it helps you to tap into the world within. How you can learn to go deeper within yourself. How you can come out of it renewed and revived. How it can bring you a sense of calm and peace of mind. Meditation, without a doubt, has a multitude of benefits that once learned and put into practice will help to center you and keep you grounded. This is so very important to communing with ourselves.

Other significant benefits to spending time alone are:
- **Reduce Depression**
- **Reduce/Eliminate Stress**
- **Center yourself**
- **Have little to no distraction**
- **Help to keep your relationships healthy**
- **Get your emotions in check**
- **Helps you to focus better**
- **Gives your creativity room to grow**
- **Connect with yourself, mind and thoughts**

- ❖ **Connect with the God within**
- ❖ **The opportunity to commune with nature**
- ❖ **Relax and unwind**
- ❖ **Revitalize your body and mind**
- ❖ **Get in touch with and awaken your soul**
- ❖ **Become super productive because you can concentrate better**

You may have thought of other reasons even while reading through this, as to why the act of being alone can be of benefit to you. The biggest thing I want you to remember is that being alone doesn't have to mean being lonely. I'm sure it will feel like that at times. I struggled with that a lot once upon a time. Well into my mid 30's, to be honest. You may find that you have to remind yourself that you are not alone. Believe this; because you are not!

Matthew 7:13-14 New International Version (NIV)

The Narrow and Wide Gates

13. "Enter through the narrow gate. For wide is the gate and broad is the road that leads to destruction, and many enter through it. 14. But small is the gate and narrow the road that leads to life, and only a few find it.

Jeremiah 6:16 New International Version (NIV)

16 This is what the Lord says: "Stand at the crossroads and look; ask for the ancient paths, ask where the good way is, and walk in it, and you will find rest for your souls. But you said, 'We will not walk in it.'

You're going to find, that as you begin making changes in your life, you may start to lose people that are in and around your circle. Some of them will be very close to you and you may find it difficult and painful to lose them. It's an unfortunate but necessary part of the process. There is a saying that speaks about allowing the people who leave your life, to do so. I can't recall it word for word, but the gist of it is this; when people choose to walk out of your life, let them.

When people walk out of your life, you allow them to leave because their departure makes room for new people to enter your life. New people, who may bring you joy and happiness. New experiences and opportunities for growth. Sometimes in trying to hold on to the people who no longer want to be a part of your life, you end up stagnating yourself. Putting your life on hold. You're keeping yourself in the very place that you want so bad to move on from. Think about it.

Also, the departure of someone out of your life isn't always a permanent one. Think of it as a leave of absence. Their absence has given you the space that you need to do what you need to do. Receive what you need to receive. Focus on what you need to focus on. You should also consider the fact that the very same opportunities will also avail themselves to the folks that have chosen to go their separate ways.

Sometimes, a person will decide to move on with their life because they also see that continuing to hold on to what's no longer serving them, is stagnating their growth as well. So a positive aspect of it all is that both sides, end up making room in their lives for something new and hopefully improved, to enter. The possibility always exists that your paths will cross again in a moment point, yet, to be discovered.

The fact of the matter is that the path less traveled is usually traveled alone. It takes discipline, self-control, motivation, a mastery that's acquired along the way, and solitude. You will be shedding people, things, habits, and beliefs that you have outgrown and are no longer serving you. You will learn to become comfortable with spending time with yourself if you're not already comfortable with it. You are taking time out for you.

It will serve you well to enter into this solitude with an open heart and mind. Be willing to see other points of view and the options that come with them. Use this time wisely, and you will begin to understand how and why the benefits are great. You will also learn, however, why few are they who can maintain a journey such as this. Have heart, dear ones. Everything you go through while on this journey is for a reason and will be well worth it. Anything worth having is worth working towards and working for. Work smart, not hard. Remember?

The development of your inner strength is a benefit of spending time with self and is an essential factor because it results in mastery of self. During this journey, you will learn to master your emotional intelligence, self-control, self-discipline, the ability to adapt and you will build resilience, which will help you to repel any and all that you choose to no longer participate in or allow in your life.

The end result of mastery of self is greater happiness, peace, fulfillment, success and mental strength. You'll find that you are more mindful of the world around you. You will have learned how to strengthen your resolve, and because of life experiences, you come to understand why you needed to.

If and when times get tough for you, while on this journey, and you find yourself feeling unbearably alone; knowing how to ease those moments of discomfort will help you to continue on your journey and do away with thoughts of doubt or giving up when you need that help most.

Some of the ways in which you can ease the discomfort that can accompany feeling bored or isolated are:

- **Busying yourself. Finding things to do that will occupy your mind and reinforce the reasons why you're traveling this path alone.**
- **Treat yourself! I mean really good! Splurge on yourself. No justification needed. You are always deserving of being treated well. The objective here is to make yourself feel good.**
- **You can go somewhere you've always wanted to go but never would before. Take a little time out for a weekend trip. Or, if the time is available for you, go all out on a 1-2 week trip and have a blast!**
- **Express yourself through the arts. You can paint, draw, write or learn to play an instrument.**
- **Think and act outside of your box. Be courageous enough to get silly sometimes.**
- **Stay positive even when it's hard to do so by changing your thoughts of negativity into a positive one.**
- **See a professional**

Seeking out help is ok. This journey isn't meant to contribute to the cause of your demise. An important reminder that I'll interject here is that these were *my* coping mechanisms as I was going through my journey. I'm merely sharing with you ways in which I used to help me through the rough times. You take what you need and do away with the rest. What I'm sharing with you are options and methods that might help you while on your personal journey.

Don't attempt to do it alone if you know you're not ready for that. Know yourself. A benefit to this all is that you come to learn yourself if you don't already. I think it's safe to say that all of us could stand to get to know ourselves a little better. We are always growing, changing and evolving.

The benefits to self from this journey are interwoven throughout this chapter. I'm sure there are many others you can think of that aren't listed. I want you also to remember that the things we do, inadvertently affect those in and around our lives as well. There is always someone watching. Regardless of how it may feel and what you may think, you are not in this alone.

At the end of the day, the path less traveled isn't an easy one. It comes with its own set of trials, tribulations, and lessons. Each journey is unique to the individual and is meant for you and you alone. The benefits outweigh the inconveniences and the inconveniences, conquered, will lend to your resolve. Your resilience. Your greater knowledge and sense of self. Your self-mastery. You have within you, the capabilities to create or destroy. You <u>are</u> <u>both,</u> the created and the creator. This journey will be everything you need it to be for you. It will do you well to remember that. You are a powerful being. This journey is meant to help you understand and live in this knowledge.

If there is something that you seek to know
That you do not yet have understanding of,
Go after the understanding
Your mind will open wide for you,
For anything, you have an <u>actual</u> interest in
And you should flow with those openings
Because that freedom in flexibility to learn
As your mind receives best
Will ultimately lead to your success

Chapter 12

Desiring From a Beggars Point of View

Desiring from a beggars point of view is precisely what the title implies. Lack of any kind is seeded by doubt that grows, seemingly uncontrollably, in the garden of your mind. You want for something you do not believe you can have and you find yourself begging and pleading for these wants whether it be by prayer or supplication. You have wants and needs. You have hopes and dreams, goals and ideas. Things that you would like to take place in your life. Things that you would like to have manifested in your life; no matter the "thing," no matter the reason. You have a desire to see and have your wants fulfilled, but you lack faith, belief, hope and trust in whether or not you'll *actually* receive what it is that you want for your life.

You're *wishing* for your wants and needs when instead, you could and should be connecting your moments to achieve them. All that you want for your life is already done. This is about taking the actions necessary in the *now*, that will lead you into the moment(s) where, what you want for your life meets with your *here and now*.

Make no mistake about it; we all have to work for what we want. We work towards the goals that we set. Short and long term goals that are meant to affect our everyday lives and provide a sense of security for our futures. However, there's a balance. It takes more than the outward, physical, hands-on work to get what you want in this life. Just as it takes more than simply thinking about what you want for your life. It'll take more than hoping and wishing for what you want in life to manifest itself. Remembering who you are and the capabilities that you possess will level you up in terms of being able to see more of what you want to be manifested and brought into fruition. Remembering, however, is just a step in the process. Acceptance and belief will play active roles in this process as well.

We are working smart . . . remember? Once again we are talking about wielding your powers. Recognizing what they are. Learning to use them properly and then allowing them to help you to live a better life. It's true, the sayings you may have heard. We were not meant to struggle in this world, this lifetime, here on this earth. None of us were. We entered this world fully equipped with everything we would need to live out this life; comfortably and abundantly.

No matter where you are in life, from this moment, the moment when you *believe* that this is true, you *can* change your life instantly and dramatically with thought alone. Yes, there will be action required; but *every*, I repeat, *every* single step we take and word we speak, starts first, with a thought.

In my experience, wishing for things to happen or come about in my life only delayed what it was that I wished for. As I reflect on it, anything that I ever "wished" for in my life, never actually came to be until I actually *did* something about it, by actioning on it to achieve what it was I was "goaling" for.

Before my mindset matured into what it is now, anything that I'd wanted in my life was wished for in one capacity or another. "I wish that I had blah, blah, blah" or "I can't wait for blah, blah, blah" or "It would be nice if blah, blah, blah." The truth is, wishing for something only confirms that you don't already have it! Saying that you can't wait, kind of has you . . . well . . . waiting. 'It would be nice' only serves to confirm the doubt in the statement. You get the picture. Our talk-speak is so very important to what we see manifested in our lives; in the now moments. Thoughts – feelings – talk-speak. This will become an essential and prevalent trio in the future. This is especially true for our desires in regards to our "future"; the moment points that we have yet to experience, yet they already are.

Just because you cannot grasp a situation, idea or spoken thought doesn't make it any less valid, possible or actual. The fact of the matter is because we create our realities on a moment to moment basis, whatever you believe or perceive your life to be, is exactly what it is. You'll have to understand the importance of perspective in this scenario. For instance, outwardly, to the world, I am not an expert on anything. This is ok by me, because I know one thing to be a matter of fact truth, I *am* an expert of me. That, ladies and gentlemen, is the only validation that I need.

Why is this so? Well aside from the fact that this book was written based on how *I* decided to take control of *my* life, as stated before in a previous chapter, to live your life according to and based on how *others* believe you should be living your life, is to operate and live this life as someone else — a puppet. You can never truly be you, trying to be what other people want you to be. There's no happiness or satisfaction in living this type of life.

It took me years, and I mean years, to understand this and apply it to my life. I didn't believe myself worthy of anything that I wanted for my life. I couldn't see that at the time, but now I know this to be true. Wanting what we believe we can't have *is* desiring from a beggars point of view. Pleading with God or the universe to "bless" you with your hearts desires, all the while you don't even have faith in your ability to be "blessed" with said desires.

Wanting what you believe you can't have doesn't eliminate the "want." Not believing yourself capable of receiving your wants, desires and a lot of times, even our needs, actually blocks our ability to receive it. We are actually limiting ourselves with this way of thinking because we're sending mixed signals. In your heart of hearts, you really do want for a specific thing. Yet, on that same token, you genuinely feel that even though you want and should have it, you're not going to get it.

The latter of the two thoughts is going to win because that's where the feeling is the strongest. Our feelings emit energy. We radiate our feelings in our immediate surroundings. That energy is capable of touching those that are around us. That energy is our aura. What are we inviting into our atmosphere, except doubt, with conflicting thoughts? Furthermore, what are we putting out into the atmosphere with these contradictory thoughts?

We deny ourselves of a more abundant life with this doubt filled envy. Keep in mind that abundance is just a considerable amount of *something*. I don't know why abundance is associated with money, finances or riches. You can have a whole lot of anything, and that anything would be what you had abundantly. For what it's worth, you can have an abundance of troubles. Not that anyone I know of would actively go looking for it. The point is that love, happiness, peace of mind, comfort and even finances can all come to us in abundance if we can rid ourselves of the envy and the doubt.

So getting to the root of this ailment is all about checking your state of worthiness. What is it to be worthy? Deserving right? When you feel worthy of something, you believe that you deserve it. What about your self-worth? How intact is it? Do you even really know? Are you dealing with self-esteem issues, yet believe that you have strong self-worth?

Listen to yourself talk sometimes. Do you find yourself in the role of the victim all of the time? Have you given up on being able to have or be anything in this life because as of this moment, you've yet to make the mark on life you believed you'd make by now? Are you feeling hopeless? Alone? Poor? Stuck? The list goes on, but for now, I want you to take each of the questions just asked and answer them in detailed entirety. Add any other connotations you associate with yourself. Confess unspoken thoughts onto that paper, letting all of that negative energy leave your body through the pen in your hand.

This is a cleansing exercise. It's a very important exercise and one that you don't want to skip. The goal here is, to rid yourself of any negative clutter that you've been carrying around. Possibly for years, you have been growing weary from the weight of this negative clutter that you have been carrying around. In truth, it's not just because you are releasing that negative energy through your fingertips, into the pen and onto the paper that you will begin to feel a shift in your being. It's because in doing this exercise there is a release, a weight lifted when we finally work up the nerve to say the things that we were once unwilling to admit to or voice out loud.

What we want at the end of this exercise is to feel lighter and to learn to see ourselves in a new light. The road to forgiveness of self is wrapped up in the releasing of negativity during the completion of this exercise. If your confidence is on shaky ground, the aim here is to solidify the foundation. Don't rush through this exercise. Take as much time as needed to complete it;

and if you find that you need to, come back to it as many times as necessary to completely release all of the negative clutter you can access within you.

With the completion of this exercise, you are reinforcing your inner strength by addressing any obstacles that may have played a part in the cause of your negativity build up in the first place. Self-doubt is a leading contender in this area. When you doubt yourself, you are putting a spin of delay on everything about your life.

You will still accomplish goals and plans in your life. You will still be able to meet your needs and wants. It will probably have taken you longer to achieve your goals and meet your needs and wants though, because self-doubt causes us to fester over and over with our thoughts and ideas, causing us to delay in taking action. Not only that, but self-doubt will also cause us to take *no* action at times which in turn, causes us to miss out on opportunities and possibilities. All because we were stuck with worry and doubt; lacking confidence in ourselves.

First things first; you will have to learn to trust yourself. Where there is a lack of trust in self, there is an inability to take full control of your life successfully. You will never have the experience you want for yourself without trust in yourself first, above all others and all things.

Next, you'll want to ground yourself and learn how to keep yourself grounded. It's essential that we learn how to live in the now. We have to stay focused on our present moment points. Remember, our past, present and future are moment points that appear to happen as sequenced events when in truth, every moment is connected from every angle or direction. This means that it is possible to get caught up in what we would consider the past. Moment points that you've already experienced but that you continuously choose to relive again and again by keeping the thought of those moments at the forefront of your mind. So staying grounded will help you to stay in the now.

You can do this by connecting with nature. Find a nice trail in your area and start going for walks or runs. Surround yourself with the trees and the breeze: the fresh air and the sun on your skin. Listen to the sound of the water running along the creek. Put your feet in the grass and feel the life from the grass and living organisms in the dirt with your toes.

You can learn to meditate. Sure, you'll probably fall asleep often in the beginning. I'm guilty of this. Truthfully, because I knew that I would fall asleep while trying to meditate, I used to reason that it wasn't for me. That was my way of justifying why I wouldn't do it. Therefore, I didn't take or make the time to actually *learn* how to do it. Not in the beginning anyway.

Meditation takes practice. You can't learn to master it if you never get started with it and the benefits you gain from it once you know how to use it, are invaluable to your peace of mind. Needless to say, I did start my practicing of meditation. To date, I am still a work in progress, and one day I *will* master it. However, that day would never come if I never even bothered to get started with it. Meditation will help to keep you centered as well as grounded. Ultimately, it will help to keep you focused.

Next, is learning to nurture yourself and keeping a balance between work, home and time for you. It can't be all work and no time for house and home or me-time. It also can't be all house and home to the detriment of your work and your "me-time"; and most certainly, you can't live with your head in the clouds. Therefore it can't be all me-time because obviously nothing else would be getting done.

Try keeping a gratitude journal. I cannot stress to you how important it is to learn to be thankful. How much you learn to appreciate the little things in this life that you've built for yourself thus far. Learning to be grateful for every little facet of your life helps you to appreciate and gain a broader perspective on just how much you *do* have. You learn to appreciate your family more. The people in your life. The roof over your head. The very air that you breathe.

Keeping a gratitude journal is a deep digging exercise in and of itself. If done with intention and given some real attention, you'll find yourself answering the what/why/because of everything you value. As well as seeing the value in things you once believed to have or hold no value in or for your life; and I'm not referring to materialistic things or things of monetary value. Although, you'll, of course, be thankful for those things as well.

Be good to yourself. Learn to treat yourself. There are many ways that you can do this. The treat is unique to the individual, but getting a massage, a spa treatment, a pedicure or going on a shopping spree are all ways you can treat yourself. It can also be as subtle as getting yourself that ice cream cone you know you've been wanting. Going to see a movie. Relaxing and taking a day off! Only you know what you need and want. You can try networking amongst family and friends. Visiting or joining a new group with like-minded individuals.

In addition to the above mentioned, I want you also to remember the following:

- ❖ Be self-forgiving. Learn to be easy on yourself. We're our worst critics.
- ❖ Failures are just lessons that teach you what *not* to do as well as aid in the development of your inner strength.
- ❖ Look for the lessons in every situation. Hit or miss. Good or bad. Not just when things go wrong.
- ❖ Learn something new.
- ❖ Pay more attention to your passions. They will lead you to your happy place.
- ❖ Celebrate yourself and your wins at every stage. Watch the successes become greater as you progress along with renewed motivation and every celebrated win you achieve at every level.

In building your trust of self and actively working towards bettering yourself, you are increasing your value to self, first, as well as those around you. You are elevating your self-worth, and I'm here to tell you it's such a great feeling! You will elevate your self-worth by:

- ❖ Getting to know yourself!
- ❖ Doing things that make you feel better.
- ❖ Doing things for others.
- ❖ Helping others who are seeking.
- ❖ Improving on yourself in ways that are specific to what you believe you lack.
- ❖ Having confidence in your ability to create for yourself/life what it is that you want.

Remember to stop worrying about the opinions of others. Opinions are just opinions, but the choice is ultimately yours! Rid yourself of any limiting fears although a little fear can be healthy. For instance, you don't want to go jumping off of any bridges or anything like that. I'm sure you get what I mean. Aside from any healthy fear, what are you afraid of? Do you trust yourself? Do you believe yourself capable of elevating your life? What's your reason for stagnation at this moment?

There is much to work through here, and I don't claim that it will be easy. It's a lot of work, and sometimes you'll feel like giving up, while other times you may feel like you're on top of the world. Still, while there are many to choose from, the one unambiguous takeaway you should get from this chapter, is that you must be armed with unwavering certainty that any and all of your desires are yours if you truly want it. Your actions will be your truth-tellers.

CHAPTER 13

It's in the Little Things

When we start to understand that in every moment of our lives, we are always living in the now, we begin to realize that life is ever truly about what we can do in the moment. It doesn't mean that we won't make plans and set goals for the moment points we have yet to connect to. It simply means that even in working towards those goals and on those plans, it's still all about taking it one step at a time because what's most important in the moment, is the moment. Each action taken has a defining moment. Every little step we take and move we make has its moment.

Therefore we should take the time to enjoy the moments in our lives. Celebrate the moments in our lives. Learn the lessons from the moments in our lives and make memories from those moments in our lives. It is after all, in the little things; because it's the little things that contribute to the whole. The bigger picture. Savor the moments. Every single one. No matter what it is you might be experiencing in any given moment. You'll wish you could live in that moment forever, or you'll be able to better appreciate, with anticipation even, the arrival of a connecting moment point.

While I was waiting for my moment points to connect, I occupied myself with whatever tasks were needing my attention at that moment. These tasks would become the building blocks for the connecting moment points. For instance, on a typical day for me, while I was still very emotional and grieving, I still found the time to write. I continued to make plans regarding my business. I always took care of my hygiene. I ate at least once a day. I don't recommend that, but I'd be remiss if I said that it wasn't hard at times just to carry out the basics of living, while I was going through those particular moment points in my life.

I made the best use of those moments that I could. I was working towards coming out of the funk that I was in. It was no cup of tea. It sounds easier than it really was, but it was not impossible. That's the important factor. It wasn't impossible, and every action I took was a step forward towards the next connecting moment. So it was progressive.

Doing things for yourself is as equally important as taking care of the tasks that you are working on to propel you towards your goals. The things you do for yourself that help to build your self-esteem and self-worth, ultimately makes you stronger and better equipped, not just for reaching your goals, but for living this life. I spoke about things in chapter 11 that could be done to treat and take care of yourself. But treating yourself isn't the same thing as building yourself and feeling confident in yourself. Believing you have and knowing your worth.

Self-esteem is about knowing how you feel and what you think about yourself. A requirement to living your best life is holding yourself in high esteem. What's your true expectancy of a successful outcome to your goals and plans, if you don't have high regard for yourself, your abilities and your capabilities? Above all else, you have to believe in yourself. So give yourself a break. Often times we can be our own worst enemy. The slack we so willingly give to others, we seem to find it difficult to convey to ourselves. Cut yourself some slack! You are, after all, living this human experience: human flaws and all.

Start paying attention to your inner voice. What are you saying to yourself? Learn how to shut down self-criticism. You can evaluate yourself, but don't overdo it. Believe it or not, much in the same way you learn to practice gratitude, you can learn to practice self-appreciation. Keep a journal and make it a point to make a daily entry about yourself. If you enter nothing else in it, make it your business to write down five things that you appreciate about yourself and why. The "why" is important. People can say a lot of things about themselves; but what's the point in having a superficial conversation with yourself?

When writing down what you appreciate about yourself, it should be easy also to write down the "why." Why list five things that you appreciate about yourself? Because eventually, you'll find yourself having to dig deeper than usual to pull out the attributes and qualities, and then of course to answer the whys. You'll find yourself going even deeper in explanation on the characteristics and qualities that you may have previously listed. Ultimately, what you'll gain from this exercise, is a more intimate, more profound connection with self. Building your esteem and solidifying confidence in yourself.

You can also try helping others. There are many ways in which you can do this, but for me, I no longer try to help people uninvited. It always seems to backfire. So instead, I make myself available to those who are wanting and asking for help. There are also soup kitchens, senior homes, family shelters and many more outlets and opportunities that will present themselves. You do what's most comfortable for you.

I'm not a believer in broadcasting what you do for others because I feel that when it's done from the heart and genuine concern or benefit of the receiver, no one needs to know except you, yourself and you! However, I want to share an incident from my twenties that was one of my most memorable 'feel good' experiences in helping someone unselfishly.

I worked at a supermarket at the time; in the front office. One morning, there was a senior woman who'd come to the desk because she'd lost her envelope with her money in it and she explained that it was the last bit of money that she'd had to purchase some groceries. She wanted to know if anyone had turned in the envelope. After checking for it in our lost and found section and checking the safe, I informed her that no one had turned in an envelope containing money.

It looked to me as if her soul just dropped out of her. She was so distraught. She looked like her world was going to end and she kept saying "what am I going to do?" Repeatedly. I felt so sorry for her. My heart cried for her as she thanked me and I watched her walk away with the woman she'd come into the store with. Then suddenly, I had an idea. So I went into the office and got an envelope and put the last thirty dollars that I had to my name in it.

I went to find her on the floor and called out to her 'Ma'am. Ma'am. I found your envelope. Someone had turned it in, and it was placed in the office. I hope it's all there.' Her eyes lit up with happiness and disbelief at the same time. That's what it looked like to me at least. She said "Oh thank you, Baby. Thank you so much! I don't know what I was going to do." Then she checked the envelope and said it was all there!

That's what blew me! I happened to have the exact amount that she'd lost, and by giving it to her, I changed her day just like that. Now some of my co-workers swore up and down I was bamboozled. While others who knew at the time, that I was robbing Peter to pay Paul, felt like I couldn't afford to do what I did. For me, however, it turned out to be one of the most memorable and gratifying feelings that I'd experienced. I had a beautiful day that day. It felt good to be able to do something for someone else for a change, and I believe that it was my foundational experience on what it should feel like to help others from that point on.

The point is, some of our best memories are composed of the little things. Day to day moments that, at the time, didn't seem like much; but for some reason, they're some of the most memorable moments that we recall. It takes work to turn your life into what you will have it to be for you, but there's no need to feel or be overwhelmed by what that ultimate goal is.

By this point in the book, you should have completed loads of exercises that were meant to be completed as you were reading along. Once again, I've only shared with you what I tried and has worked for me, in the hopes that it might be able to help someone else. I know from experience, all too well, that at times this will feel like much too much work. It might even seem redundant at times, but repetition breeds mastery.

Up to now, we've addressed:
- **Our thoughts and how they shape our reality**
- **Making decisions and taking action on them**
- **Soul searching and digging deep within for answers**
- **Answering lots of hard questions about ourselves**
- **Setting goals and coming up with action plans that we actually work on**

- ❖ Looking at how we block and stagnate our lives at times and changing bad habits
- ❖ The importance of having a strong and confident view of ourselves
- ❖ Facing our personal truths
- ❖ The power we have within
- ❖ Learning how to let go of thoughts, ideas, behaviors, and beliefs that are no longer serving us
- ❖ Taking full responsibility for our lives
- ❖ How and why we shouldn't judge or allow ourselves to be judged by others
- ❖ Accessing our inner capabilities and recognizing ourselves for who and what we truly are
- ❖ Learning to wield our power for our greater good
- ❖ Being mindful of the way we speak to and about others. As well as to and about ourselves and our lives
- ❖ The benefits of being adaptable and dealing with change
- ❖ The benefits of solitude and how to use it to our advantage
- ❖ How to believe in what we want for ourselves and manifest quicker
- ❖ Taking things day by day and celebrating the growth as we go along

There should already, at this point, be a renewed sense of self. A better understanding of self. Some self-actualization that has you, even now, feeling like a different person. More like a new and improved version of you. Remember that we are taking this one day at a time. Working on it little by little. Whatever that may be for you. You move at the pace that works for you. Being mindful not to slip into old habits that did not serve you.

In the coming chapters, we'll look at how we can:
- ❖ **Turn our goals into a plan and then work on those plans to meet our goals**
- ❖ **Free ourselves from self-imposed bondage**

- ❖ Consider new ways of perceiving and understanding things as it relates to time; and how it pertains to our decisions and actions that we take
- ❖ Pinpoint the pivots of living this life and explore how we can apply them to our everyday living
- ❖ Bridge the gap and help others. As well as how we can be a part of helping others to break free from their invisible chains, to achieve their highest levels of living this life

Effort. It doesn't take much, and yet the end result will be so significant and wondrous, that it'll appear as though you've toiled your entire life. When in truth, you've just essentially, taken each day by the day. Moment by moment. Celebrating each moment for the successes and the lessons. Until one day you turned around and noticed, that you've accomplished a multitude of goals that once seemed so far away and at times unattainable. It's in the little things.

CHAPTER 14

Mapping Out the Master Plan

Ask any successful person, and they'll tell you, they had a plan of some sort. Even if the details weren't completely mapped out right away, their success is due, in part, to the fact that a plan was created and then worked on until what they were goaling for was achieved. A plan, after all, is just a bunch of thoughts, dreams, and ideas brought together in an orderly fashion, meant to play out as a sequence of events that will inevitably lead to the end goal. Every successful manifestation of an achieved goal started first, with a thought.

So first things first, if you can conceive it and you believe <u>with</u> <u>your</u> <u>heart</u> that you will achieve it, then you *will* receive it! Plain and simple. We are born equipped with the ability to do anything that we can think of. If you're not rocket ship inclined, you're not going to be having thoughts about how to build a rocket ship. However, were the opposite true and you were inclined towards rocket science then, within your make-up would exist already, a deeply seeded, un-flowered idea on how to build rocket ships, in the form of a thought yet to be born.

We are not a one size fits all species. We were not all encoded with the same genes. We are a part of a collective, yes; but each with our own individuality as well. We each carry our own unique make-up that's a part of our identity. This degree of separation is one of the reasons why we can excel as a species to heights unimaginable. Provided we honed into our individual abilities and used them for the greater good of the collective.

Think about two people. A couple if you will. Each of the two, equipped with their individual specialties, abilities, and capabilities, that when blended, will heighten their shared qualities and make stronger the couple as a whole. Together, they complement each other. What one is lacking, the other brings to the table and together the two are one unified force. Their differences combined, increases their possibilities because the thoughts, dreams, and ideas are unique to the individual.

But working collectively, however, their thoughts, dreams, and ideas are bouncing off of each other, creating possibilities that they may never have conceived of individually. If our thoughts, dreams, and ideas were all the same, we'd create nothing new outside of what we knew as a collective.

You may have heard it said, "Not everyone can do everything." Then again you have people, including myself, chiming on about how we can do anything we want to do. Both are true within these margins: anything that we can think of, we *can* do. The caveat being that we have to have a belief in our ability to do it; including ideas presented or introduced to you by someone else. If there's a genuine interest, you'll find that you can bring any idea to life. You wouldn't be able to do anything that you couldn't visualize yourself doing.

We're not talking about likability either. Nor are we talking about not doing a thing, just because you don't like it or maybe you feel it's beneath you. That's not what we're talking about here. We're talking about taking a job performing a task you've never done before but had within you the ability to learn how to do it. That is to say that we *are* capable of learning *anything*. It's a matter of setting your mind to learn a given task and then mastering the ability to do it. The only things you don't know how to do are the things that you *don't want* to do.

We're talking about the fact that because we are beings of energy our paths to individuality are attracted to us very much in the same way that we are attracted to it. These paths ignite thoughts, dreams, and ideas that become expressions of our individuality. These expressions then, in turn, light fire to our aspirations, motivation, determination, and perseverance. They are giving strength to our will and commitment to seeing our thoughts and ideas manifested into goals and plans and in turn, receiving the satisfaction of success after seeing your goals met, as your plans come to fruition.

Mapping out your master plan has nothing to do with who you think you are, and everything to do with who you don't even know yourself to be as of yet. If you haven't already done so; in your notebook or workbook that you should've began when you started this book, you should have already written down somewhere in the top of your list, getting to know yourself. Finding out who you are. You will not be able to stand firm on anything you attempt to do, if you do not first, know who you are.

Let's go over a bit of why and how increasing our thinking abilities, expands our possibilities. For starters, I'll give an example of what I'm trying to convey. If you don't know about the existence of a place, how can you ever aspire to go? If you've never heard of Einstein (not likely but we'll use the example anyway), what would prompt you to study his life? His research? His findings?

We are more than the human being that we see ourselves as, but we are still human beings; and because of this, we have to meet the needs of these bodies that we inhabit. We're supposed to live this life experience to its fullest and enjoy every bit of it that's there to give or rather, that's there for the taking. To do this, we must expose ourselves to as much as possible to gain experience and knowledge and even wisdom along the way. In doing this, we are feeding our souls, nurturing them even. While the human being that you represent in this life is also enjoying or suffering, but either way learning, from these same experiences.

So imagine knowing to be true, at a very young age and with a full understanding of what it means, when you are told that the world is yours. Imagine knowing how to request of your higher self, the aid you need in the now, by using your heart to do so. Imagine being able to take the world by storm and making the fullest of your life from a very young age. How fulfilling would that be?! Pay attention to the times because that is what our world is evolving into.

However, since we didn't start in the direction that the newer generations are going, we're going to start where we are now. There is nothing like the present, and the present is all there is. Do you want to expand your possibilities in the now? Start increasing your thinking abilities. Expose yourself to the nouns of life. People, places, things that you've never seen, interacted with or been before.

- ❖ Read books
- ❖ Explore the internet
- ❖ Look up cities in other countries and learn about them
- ❖ Choose to learn about something you don't like
- ❖ Join a group geared towards an interest of yours
- ❖ You can learn a new language and then take a trip or go somewhere where you can put it to use
- ❖ You can study another culture
- ❖ Learn a new word and the multiple ways in which you can use that one word
- ❖ You can learn about the stars, their systems, and the universe

There is no limit to the possibilities. The only limit is yourself. The more you expose yourself to, the more you expand your mind and ways of thinking. Your thoughts will begin to fill with content that, once upon a time, would not have occupied your mind space. You'll find yourself dreaming about some of what you learn. You'll find your sub-conscious revealing to you wonders and ideas you may never have even imagined before, had you not been exposing yourself to the nouns of life.

Think of all of the possibilities that you expose yourself to, just by choosing to keep your mind stimulated. It doesn't take much to learn something new. The benefit of which will broaden your horizons like never before. This is also where mapping out a master plan, from this point forward if you have not already done so, will arm you for success.

It's not enough to expose yourself to possibilities. None of it matters if you're not willing to take action on any of it. What good is it to know a bunch of information and gaining exposure to possibilities if you never plan on using any of it? Why even bother acquiring it from the get-go? If you're going to go through the motions, take the time and make an effort to do all of these things, what's the master plan?

There is and should always be an ultimate goal. What is that for you? You will need to define what that ultimate goal is for you. Mapping out the master plan will take some effort, but will be well worth it. You'll go through your long and short term goals. You'll be organizing and prioritizing them. You'll break your long term goals into shorter termed goals. Creating from those short term goals, a mini set of action plans of which you can act on; gaining satisfaction and the feeling of success at every win as each plan is completed and for every goal reached. All of this will happen on a continual roll as you work towards the master plan.

You don't want to overwhelm yourself by taking on your master plan dead on. That's the reason why it's better to break it down into short term goals. Your master plan will have a big bang effect. Causing significant, positive changes in your life, that you should be expecting; and you will, therefore, have to put in some major work connecting your moment points. A lot of folks attempt to take on the master plan all at once. It's unnecessary. The results aren't visibly immediate, and it can be intimidating, discouraging and disappointing.

However, if you break your master plan down into smaller sets of goals, you'll find greater satisfaction and fulfillment in working towards your master plan because you'll be able to see and celebrate in the moment, the mini-triumphs. All of which inevitably leads to the major triumph.

- ❖ Set goals
- ❖ Create a plan
- ❖ Work the plan to its successful completion
- ❖ Repeat

That's all there is to it. Every mini set of goals completed brings you that much closer to the completion of the master plan! It'll take discipline, determination and focus but you can do it. It'll require you to put your best foot forward and again; you can do it. Nothing is impossible, and there is only the now. Any and everything that you want to do, you can! Today you're deciding to get out there and live the best life you can live! Set your goals and make your plans, then have fun with it and celebrate the successes as you watch your master plan come to fruition, one mini goal at a time!

CHAPTER 15

Worthiness, Forgiveness, Acceptance & Accountability

The questions you're asking yourself, and the process of digging deep that you're going through is all for the purpose, of finding your true self and being able to stand firm in who you are. You have to believe in yourself. How can you do that if you don't know who you are? Knowing, understanding and believing in who you are, gives you a firm foundation on which to stand.

This decision you've made or that you are in the midst of making is a chance to start new and refreshed; freer than ever before and with nothing but success to look forward to because you will have worked for it. You will have earned it, and it doesn't take a lifetime to achieve.

The answers you'll inevitably come upon in this chapter should help to confirm and then fortify your feeling and understanding of your worthiness. You are worthy of having and living the life that you want. You are worthy of being happy and living free. You are worthy of having the most fulfilling human experience possible. Any and everything is yours for the taking. It's all up to you.

Knowing what it is that you genuinely want and being willing to go after it, is an essential factor in all of this as well. Anything that we genuinely want seeps from within us. We will reek of it simply because it becomes a part of us until it is received or achieved. Once attained, there's contentment for some and on to the next phase for others. Limitations exist only in the mind. Lack can be overcome with planning, strategizing, seeking, resourcing and doing. Feeling worthy will give you the motivation to go after any and everything you want.

Whenever you bump into a stumbling block, don't try to ignore it by skipping over it, waiting and getting back to it later or giving up! Instead, you should work it out as soon as possible. Get help if you need to, but clear it up. It's not impossible, and that's always what you should remind yourself of during those times; especially when it's a difficult stumbling block, you're working to get through. Remember, everything you need to succeed is within you, but sometimes it can be difficult to see this because unprocessed emotions can blind us. Therefore, before you can truly begin to feel worthy of anything, you'll need to address any reason(s) that may exist leading you to feel unworthy.

Worthiness

- ❖ **What is it to feel worthy?**
- ❖ **Do you feel worthy of having and living this life?**
- ❖ **Do you feel worthy of having a *successful life?**

*Success is defined as the accomplishment of an aim or a purpose

Can you see with more than your eyes? Are you limiting your vision to only what you can see with your natural eyes? Have you ever considered or do you now use your feelings to see? For instance, your intuition, gut feeling or just a *knowing*. Do you trust those feelings? How often do you rely on them?

The quality of our lives and one of the ways we measure success is to compare it to what we value and believe. Perception is everything where this is concerned. We should also take into consideration that the factors surrounding us, will influence our perception. Just as our life's circumstances will come to influence what we value and believe. None the less, your perception about the quality of your life, and the way you measure your success, is the only version that matters. Most especially, when others may object to, or can't understand, the way you *see* things.

Feeling worthy is a part of the make-up of your foundation, and it will help you to stand firm in who you are. That being said, let's address any unprocessed emotions that will bonafidely get in the way of your feeling worthy of anything.

Forgiveness

Forgiveness is a tricky process. It involves the processing of emotions that made you feel a certain way and then choosing to let go and release those emotions to move on. It usually consists of the forgiving of another individual. However, it's almost always about forgiving yourself. It's not always easy to do, and sometimes it's a false forgiving. Meaning you *think* you forgave someone only to find out later on down the line that you haven't, after noticing that they can still evoke emotions within you that are out of your control. Forgiving yourself gives you more room and freedom, in your heart and mind, to forgive others. Experience, however, has caused me to conclude that self-forgiveness has proven to be one of the more difficult processes to go through.

First and foremost, forgiveness is all about you. Whether you are dealing with having to forgive others or with forgiving yourself, forgiveness is for you. Holding on to feelings such as hurt, pain, revenge, rage and any other emotions that keep you in a place of turmoil, only serve to hold *you* back. After all, you're the one who'll walk around harboring these unprocessed emotions that have you acting and feeling some type of way. Meanwhile, the person or persons with whom you have unresolved issues, is unbothered, free and clear, because your emotions have nothing to do with them.

So what is it to forgive yourself? What does that mean exactly? Simply put, to forgive yourself is to release yourself. What you are freeing yourself from is a self-imposed prison of the mind, reinforced by the matters of your heart. Fueled by your thoughts manifested into pain. You set yourself free when you forgive yourself because once you have fully acknowledged and accepted your self-forgiveness, you will then have the freedom to move in any direction of your choosing without any invisible blockers that were keeping you in bondage.

In keeping with the idea of free will, the understanding of what it affords you should arm you with a degree of confidence. It's because of free will that you're in control of your life at all times; Even when it doesn't seem like it. You have a choice in every situation you face. You are choosing to go in one direction or the other, deciding to take one action or another. There's always another option, no matter the choice you are making. I'll admit, the choices aren't always ideal. Sometimes none of the solutions or options to choose from seem to be the answer. Still, even in choosing to do nothing, you have made a choice. But you see, this is yet another example of how we are in control of every aspect of our lives. Every single decision we make, no matter the circumstances or the situation, demonstrates this power because control is a form of power. Self-control is a very powerful tool of which we should all arm ourselves with.

Albeit, it's harder to forgive ourselves than it is to forgive others, seemingly, because I don't believe it possible to truly be able to forgive another when you can't truly forgive yourself. How can you? You'd be ill-equipped. Just as in the idea or ability to love someone; you have to know how to love yourself and be in the constant practice of loving yourself to really be able to love another. Otherwise what you *believe* to be love or forgiveness, in this case, is just a mental bandage on a much bigger problem.

Remembering, in the words of Lisa Nichols, that "Energy grows where energy flows," you'll want to address, head on, any internal issues that are sitting unresolved because you've been avoiding processing thru them. Unless you'd rather be a slave to your past, this is an essential part of your growth. So while you will want to go deep in order to get to the source of whatever deep-rooted, unresolved emotions you may be holding on to, you don't want to feed the negativity by holding on or dwelling in those negative thoughts and emotions any longer than you need to, in order to process the "why?" After all, the point in this process is to forgive yourself.

If by chance you find that this task is more than you can handle alone, please consult with a professional and get aid in going through this process. I can make no claims on how things will go for each, individual who has the guts to go through this process and face, head on, the "ugly." I will say, that it has the potential to cause great pain before you actually make it through to the freedom that you are seeking. Having a professional to help you through this might prove to be in your best interest. Only YOU will know what's right for you.

Also, choose wisely. Professionals are human beings just as we are. They've gone through the schooling and gained some knowledge and experience in helping others, and some are very good at it, but they are still human beings just the same and therefore subject to the fallacies of being so, which means, interjecting their feelings and beliefs into situations. Common practice may work for the average man, but you are so much more than that!

You have a knowledge and understanding that has not yet availed itself to every human being on the earth thus far. You have the ability and the right to choose who and what works for you. Likewise, there is nothing wrong with interviewing someone and being specific about what it is that you want to work on and would like help with. Maintain control at all times.

Forgiving yourself and others will allow you to release, learn and grow. You should be processing with a plan in place. Do not do it alone if you don't feel capable of doing so. Processing raw, unfiltered emotions can be very painful. Sometimes a lot more than a person can bear. Don't be afraid to seek help if you need it. Remember to love yourself in the *now*! This process is going to help you to grow closer to yourself by building and developing a more intimate knowing of you. Keep your eye on the prize!

When forgiving others, you're taking into consideration how they've wronged you and how it made you feel. You're also considering how much they may or may not mean to you and whether you believe them *worth* having in your life. You'll also want to consider whether you'll be able to go forward with this person because forgiving doesn't mean forgetting. No matter the transgression, if you have to continually forgive someone every time you think of how they wronged you, then you have not truly forgiven them, and perhaps, you may need to cut ties. However, before cutting ties, have you forgiven yourself? Could that be the reason you can't go forward? We don't, all of the time, think of the fact that we're angry with ourselves and therefore we need to forgive ourselves as well, for the actions of another. Let me explain.

How often have you felt that you could "kick yourself" for something that happened where you wished you could have made a different choice? What about being angry with yourself because you decided to trust someone and they betrayed you? How about feeling sad or mad about something you may have done to another? You see, whether you've betrayed the trust of another or have had your trust betrayed, you'll still have to forgive yourself to truly be free and clear to move on. Like I said before, you can't truly forgive someone else without first forgiving yourself.

To do this, open yourself up to feeling. You're going to have to be willing to *feel* whatever emotions are holding you back. These are the emotions described in the previous paragraph although they're not limited to what's been described above. You are allowing yourself to feel the pain to get it out of your system so that you can be free of it. Let me mention again, and probably not for the last time, that it's ok to seek out help to help you get through this. The processing of some of these emotions can be daunting and hard. It's not as easy for some as it is for others, this I know, but it's not impossible, and that's what I'm trying to impress upon you.

Forgive yourself so that you're not living as a prisoner in your mind. Forgive yourself because holding on will only serve to harden your heart and make you bitter. Forgive yourself because you deserve to have the best human experience possible. Forgive yourself because tomorrow isn't promised to anyone. Forgive yourself so that you can forgive others. Forgive yourself because freedom lies on the other side. You are in control. Use your power! Control is power, and you are in control of your life! Therefore you have the power. Use it!

Acceptance & Accountability

Maya Angelou said it best, "When people show you who they are, believe them." I have found that dealing with folks is so much simpler when you accept them for who they are; The good, the bad and the ugly. How you choose to interact with people is entirely up to you. Who you decide to keep in your life is again, entirely up to you. Who you build your circles with is entirely up to you. Bottom line, no one decides on how you'll deal with a person except you. Keep in mind that this isn't limited to just dealing with people. It also applies to situations and circumstances that we face in our lives. Acceptance doesn't mean settling. Acceptance is your response to things for what they are without adding to or taking away from what it is that you are actually seeing, getting or perceiving. Ultimately, it's your actions that will determine the outcome.

When you accept folks for who they are, you can eliminate disappointment from unmet expectations. The same can be said about the situations and circumstances that we deal with in our lives as well. When our expectations go against what we get in life or does not match up with what has been shown to us, it can lead to disappointment.

By accepting people for who they are, you are giving them the freedom to be themselves. Freedom of expression inevitably leads to growth. This is in part, how we learn. Just as we have learned from our experiences and our ability to live this life in the way in which we desired, so too should others have the opportunity to do the same. Keeping in mind that age doesn't dictate growth. It works in direct correlation with physical growth, sure; but the degree to which someone grows in the mind is determined by our surroundings, rearing, experiences and education (formal or otherwise). Anyone can gain knowledge, but wisdom is acquired from going through, not sucking out.

Knowledge and wisdom aren't the same. Many of us already know this, but there are some who have not yet figured this out, so bear patience with what you'd consider being redundant statements and explanations. Experience is the wisdom "teacher." We are also built with a *knowing*. We are equipped with abilities we haven't even recognized or begun to understand yet, much less be able to put to use. The "know-how" is already within us. It's all about getting to the point of understanding beyond our current perception and beliefs.

Your interactions with others give you the opportunity to observe them. You are *learning* them and learning from them. Once you educate yourself with who a person is, you can then choose how you deal with them.

Incorporating the wisdom you've gained from *your* life experiences, you are now able to have a care-free relationship or acquaintance with whomever you choose in whatever capacity you choose and on whatever level you deem appropriate. Leaving very little room for disappointment; and because it will be on your terms, if you do find yourself disappointed, you'll be able to accept it for what it is, take responsibility for your part and forgive yourself so that you can move on. That's accountability. Don't forget to take with you, the lesson(s) learned from each experience.

In regards to accountability where it relates to self, you're taking responsibility for your actions, the results of those actions you've decided to make and your life as it is and where it is at any given point in time. Going forward, you are going to be taking responsibility for every aspect of your being. You'll be able to assess yourself, picking out what's good and expanding on it. Identifying the parts of you that you don't like, accepting that this is who you are or have been up until now, and then changing the parts that you don't like. Only *you* can do this! You have to know, feel and believe this.

If you rely on others to tell you what to change, you'd be perpetrating a fraud to yourself and others. The change won't be long-lasting, and you could end up with contempt brewing inside of you because you're living a life defined and designed by others, that may not be what or where you want to be. If you find yourself identifying with the feedback of others, *you* are to take responsibility and hold yourself accountable; making any necessary changes that *you* deemed to be important and *for your* greater good.

Summing up: You *are* worthy of having and living a successful life. If you're feeling unworthy, you'll need to assess why that is and then work on the forgiving process since you are accountable to yourself. Once you have worked out the whys and you've forgiven yourself; armed with a new outlook, you should be able to accept things for what they are. Recognizing that you have control; you have the power to catapult your life to the level of success you feel worthy of! You are now at the helm. Take control of the wheel!

CHAPTER 16

The Perception of Time

Time is a finicky subject because, to truly explore the possibilities with a completely open-mind, we'll have to fight against our time-related belief system, to gain understanding and to be able to accept what we come to learn and understand about time as it indeed is. Currently, the world as we know it operates on linear time. Under the general consensus, our perception of time stems from the belief that our lives are a sequence of events that happen in a, one way, forward moving direction.

Time is but an illusion, incorporated into the lives of the human species to aid in giving structure to our lives. We live within a time-based construct broken down into dates; days, hours, minutes, seconds. Going further, we even choose to differentiate the past, present and future, all for the sake of creating and keeping some sort, of order. A necessity at first, as we were less advanced and ill-equipped to process the concept of subjective time in this constrictive human form.

However, as we evolve as a species and we learn to tap into our God-given abilities, knowledge, and understanding, we are finding the construct of time to be more of a restrictive prison of sorts. One that keeps us just one locked door away from being able to live freely in the freedom that will be ours, with the real understanding of subjective time.

The subject of time can be a book on its own, but for the purposes of this book, I would like to discuss specifically, how the construct of linear time, limits the potential of the human race; consciously and subconsciously. It'll seem a little hard for some, to wrap your heads around conceptually, but if you choose to read with an open mind, you may come to see why I believe there is validity in the concept of subjective/simultaneous time.

So before you go any further, I want you to take a moment to prepare your mind to be open to the possibilities by stating your beliefs on and what you know about time. Be sure that it's clear to you. Most of us don't think about this on a regular or everyday basis, so you'd be surprised to learn that you might not be able to articulate your understanding of time as you believe in it now. Once you've done this, however, I want you to release it. Meaning, clear the slate by packing up your belief, so to speak, and temporarily putting it away to make room for the possibilities to occupy that space in your mind. Do this for the sake of being open, to fully ponder, feel and explore life from the perspective of subjective time.

For the sake of clear understanding; with linear time it's pretty simple. Our lives progress sequentially. That is, every step of our lives goes one step after the other, with each step affecting the next in a forward moving timeline. Meaning, we cannot go back in time, nor can we go any further ahead in time than the very next step. In Linear time, we operate by way of cause and effect. Our past affects our present and our actions in the present determines our future.

With subjective time, time can be viewed, approached, lived and felt from a variety of points of view and locations and all simultaneously. Our feelings, beliefs, and intuition play an active part in our views where subjective time is concerned. With subjective time, we only ever live in the moment, and our actions and emotions help to determine which <u>moment</u>; not which *timeline* we are in, but which <u>moment</u> we are *experiencing.*

In working towards gaining a better understanding of subjective time, we'll come to learn of and put into use, the merging of our inner comprehension, which is inherent to our higher selves, with our physical selves. Thereby controlling our worlds and the world around us, as we see it, live it, feel it and interact with it. How we perceive time, dictates what we will do with it.

Time works with you, not against you. We, in turn, have to learn to work *with* time and not against it but to do this, we must first have a better understanding of it. Time perceived from the point of view of abundance, as in I have all the time in the world, gives you all the time needed to carry out a multitude of tasks in a given day, timeframe or period. However, time perceived from the point of lack, as in you never have enough time, will only leave you feeling less accomplished because there just wouldn't be enough time in a day, timeframe or period to complete your tasks.

Getting a grip on time, as it relates to the content of this book, is essential to successfully act out any of the plans that you've decided on. No matter the size of the task or where it stands on your list of priorities, you'll still need the time to make it happen.

Now, stay with me if you will. Time *is* a control mechanism — no ifs, and or buts about it. We lead our lives according to time. Every day is directed by time. We measure our success, in part, by time. Time holds strong importance in our human lives. This is precisely why we should have a better understanding of its inner workings and how it affects our lives. This knowledge and new understanding should only help to enhance the quality of your life; no matter where you are in this life. Learning to bend time to your will affords you the opportunity to make better use of the time you'll gain through this new ability that you've tapped into.

I think it's important to remember that we are far more than our physical make-up. Explorers, if you will. Entities comprised of consciousness. We are ever evolving with each, individual quest. It's hard to fathom for some, and easy to forget by others who actually acknowledge and accept this belief. It's so easy to get caught up in living this life, that we forget the ultimate point of it all. The <u>experience</u>, in any given moment, *is* the point of it all! Rich or poor, dull or bright; the quality of your experiences while on this earth is entirely up to you!

Having a better understanding of linear and subjective time and the effect they have on our lives, upon belief, allows us to be more successful and productive, consciously and subconsciously, in every moment of our lives. Because once understood, we are empowered to make better decisions based on perspectives previously unavailable to our mind's eye and psyche.

The ability to perceive life according to subjective time was always there. It is blocked, from our mind's eye point of view, where we couldn't see it because we'd yet to tap into it. Tapping in requires first, learning about it. We purposely learn for understanding. We also learn, by happenstance, from the lessons that will come our way at some point in our simultaneous moments.

All in all, there has to be an understanding that encompasses not only comprehension but also *acceptance* and *believing*. You see, without belief, it simply does not exist. Point, blank, period.

Therefore, navigating time once learned and put into practice will allow you to regulate and control it, subconsciously. Only in the beginning, will you have to work at it consciously. Your outward or external experience will be this newfound sense of freedom. Freedom comes on many levels and through many outlets that are the aspects of our lives. Keep this in mind, for those of you looking for 'snap of the finger' miracles.

Our minds, on a conscious level, are limited in their ability to see past what we *know* unless we *will* it to do otherwise. So operating in subjective time takes acceptance, learning, and practice. We are accepting that it *is* possible. We are learning *how* to wield it and then putting that training into practice, consciously, until your subconscious takes over. You *have* to believe this if you are to learn to master it.

From my understanding, of which I am still in training on, with subjective time, we are living all of our moment points simultaneously. Therefore believing in and living life according to subjective time, frees the mind from the thought of lack of time and even the fear of death. Another point of view to the concept of death is that we are consciousness and the conscious never dies. We only shed the host shells we inhabited when taking human form. Once the "shell" expires, consciousness moves on. Under this theory, of which I hold a strong belief in, we do not die. We only level up; moving on to the next phase of our conscious existence, therefore eliminating the fear of dying. None of which, is controlled by time as we know it here on this plane.

Lucid dreaming, for example, is a form of freedom outside of the construct. The construct being linear time and the way that we process cause and effect. In a lucid dream, once we realize that we're dreaming, we're in control. We can take control of a dream, the minute we realize that we're dreaming and that we *can* change the outcome of any situation happening within our dream. Imagine then, if this same concept is applied to our waking, conscious lives. We'd be taking control of our monotonous lives.

Our subconscious holds a lot of our power; but seeing as how we are conscious, sentient beings, it just makes sense that the ultimate goal would be for that power to be realized in our conscious wake.

Our dreams are where the subconscious is awake and in full control. Operating under this theory, understanding and using lucid dreaming, subjective and simultaneous time is the key to unlocking your constricted life. It will become a way to step outside of the box and gain a new perspective. We are taking a look, from the outside in, with the understanding that we are creating our reality with every conscious thought and subconscious belief.

My experience has been, that time is not our friend when we are going through something that causes pain or heartache. For example, have you ever noticed that when things are going well in your life, time seems to pass by all too quickly, but when you are going through and dealing with hardship, time all but comes to a halt? The culprit here is time. Like a warden, it holds the key to this self-imposed prison that we choose to be restricted by. While on the same token, it's the key to healing quicker, physically and emotionally. Also the key, to making better decisions and living a more fruitful life. This chapter aims to show you how to take the "reigns" of time and wield it to your will; your control.

The sky is *not* the limit. There is no limit to who or what we can be in this life, on this earth, while we are here. Do you want to take control of the reigns of time in your life? Here's how:

- ❖ **Make the best and most use of your "time" during the day by eliminating the restriction of timeframes in your daily life. An example of doing this would be to map out or write down everything you want to accomplish that day, prioritizing the order in which you'll achieve it and then just doing it. Do not allow time to be a factor in what you are working on.**
- ❖ **If you know nothing about lucid dreaming, make it your business to do so. By doing so, you can learn to accomplish some of your "to do" list in your dreams! Seriously! Yes, yes, yes; you'll, of course, have to**

physically carry out some of what's required, in your wake, but you'd be surprised how your dreams can help you to take care of things while you're asleep. Not to mention all of the traveling you can do. All while your body is resting!

- ❖ Pay attention to your dreams. There are lots of answers, solutions, and ideas that come to you by way of your dreams. I suggest you keep a dream journal right next to your bed so that you can write about it as soon as you awake from it. <u>Before</u> turning the lights on, looking at the clock or giving thought to anything other than what you were just involved in right before you awake, you should be writing.
- ❖ Practice *feeling* your moments and experiences. Your feelings will aid your mind in "traveling" to your moment points. You've got a project that you want to see completed? *Feel* the completion of that project and ride in the visual those feelings give you. Having a desire that you'd like to see manifested and actually having it come into fruition is only a matter of one moment-point working its way to the other.
- ❖ Don't be afraid to use your imagination. It's not just for children. Think about who is the most free-spirited in this world. Kids who are not yet tarnished by the restrictions or rules to living this life; and elders, who finally got to the point of understanding that a lot of the "rules" they based their lives around, they could have done without.
- ❖ Dream the impossible dream! Don't limit yourself on your capabilities in this life. You can do *anything* you want to do, and earth plane realistic has nothing on your consciousness existence!

We were born, all of us, with all of the same make-up and capabilities as the higher up(s) who created us, but without instructions on how to use our abilities to their fullest potential.

As a Seth reader (content that simply resonates with my soul), I have come to understand and believe that we are indeed a fragment of our whole. With all of the same qualities and abilities (properties if you will) as that of our entity or higher selves. Only, these abilities lie dormant and unused until we come to know of them, accept and believe that we *actually* have them, and then learn how to tap into these abilities and put them to use.

We have this power, and learning how to use it and then actually using it *is* power in and of itself! A profound discovery for some. Powerful in its own right! Knowing that you can change the course of your life by adjusting your perspective on time! Phenomenal! Simply phenomenal!

CHAPTER 17

Trust, Faith, Hope & Believing

We can't be afraid of dreaming the impossible dream. Even more important, we cannot be afraid to carry out the vision. From our human perspectives, the impossible is unachievable. For there is something within those, who believe this to be true, that hinders their ability to see past the "blockers," making the impossible unachievable. But I dare say that it's in the impossible that everything is possible. It is, being able to go after what you want even when you can't fully see the end result. It's taking risks where others might play it safe or going the extra mile when you're ready to give in because you know that the goal you seek is at the finish line.

This human state of being is a temporary experience lived out in a shell. These shells, our bodies, are a temporary form of housing for an even greater entity within. As such, our human personas are in no way a reflection of who and what we truly are. They are instead, ego-centered, vessels of passage, which are used to participate in this learning experience called life. It is only in this human form that we even bother to acknowledge and choose to be limited by the term "impossible."

Acknowledging, accepting and believing in this fact (nothing is impossible), eliminates a considerable portion of the negative attachments that we subconsciously carry in our thoughts. Nothing is impossible. Like an underlying tone that we cannot hear, yet still it affects the fabric of our being;

Trust, faith, hope and believing are all key intertwining attributes for living this life. Think about that for a second.

Name any day in your life where you have not had to rely on one or the other or even all, within and throughout the day. You *hope* you have a good day. You *believe* it's going to be a great day. You have *faith* that your day will go well. You *trust* that this day is going to be your best yet! You can apply any of those words to a multitude of situations and circumstances that we face daily. Whether you know it or not, you are acting on one, some, or all of these, every single day.

Automated application. You know the words, and by definition, you understand the meaning of each. It doesn't take much of a conscious effort to act on any of these since acting on one, inevitably, leads to you acting on the others. Therefore, you apply it to your circumstances and situations without a second thought. Let me explain.

To <u>trust</u> something or someone is to have <u>faith</u> in a <u>belief</u> in regards to that something or someone. That belief can be connected to hope. Since hoping for something is indirectly believing that something is possible and choosing to have trust or faith in that belief. I don't believe that we, as human beings, believe in anything that we deem impossible.

That almost looks like trickery of words, but if you look again, you'll find truth. Trust is an automated response to the repetition of some form of behavior that lends itself to a level of comfort, held by the individual doing the trusting. Your belief fuels that trust. Believing in something or someone triggers that feeling of comfort needed to have this feeling of trust.

Now I want you to think about trusting yourself to make decisions, and the role that belief plays in being able to trust yourself. Do you really trust yourself to do anything that you don't believe yourself capable of doing? Do you have faith in your abilities? How about hope? Hoping that you'll be able to execute and complete a task? Even your hope is set on a weak foundation if you don't have faith in your abilities. Can you see where I'm coming from? Can you see where I'm going with this?

Hope sits in a tricky little spot. It can be based on faith, where you have confidence in receiving what it is that you are hoping for and are therefore hoping for it with an expectation of manifestation. Or it can be based in doubt, where you can be hoping for something with the expectation that what you are hoping for, will fail to manifest itself for you. Your mindset plays a critical part, where hope is concerned. Your mindset lends itself to your feelings. Regardless of what we tell ourselves and even what we say out of our mouths, if we don't feel it, it's not real.

"Now faith is the substance of things hoped for, the evidence of things not seen." Hebrews 11:1 King James Version (KJV)

In other words, when we are hoping for something and have a firm belief that what we are hoping for will be manifested. We project confidence with a firm conviction in what it is that we are hoping for, based on that belief. In fact, your faith in a person, thing or situation can even activate your will. The will to do whatever you need to, so that what it is you have faith in and are hoping for, would come to fruition.

We do all of this without any proof of its possibility. Faith is like the glue that holds hope together; connecting that hope with trust and belief — creating a feeling within you that aids in bringing about (by way of energy) the expected results. The results you were hoping for. Many of us are familiar with the power of *feeling* something that you trust and believe in. You allow yourself to open up to, receive and live, as though whatever you are hoping for has already come to pass. This experience cannot be achieved by words alone, but *it is* very much, achievable. Anything you believe, you can achieve; but you must also feel it and work towards it. What you are feeling, is a direct response to the outcome of what you were hoping for, manifested in the now. As if, from the moment you had the thought, the end result appeared immediately.

This journey you have begun, from the moment you made your decision, if worked on with intention and perseverance, will help you to gain a better understanding of self. By the time you have reached this chapter, you should already have done some serious work. Working on each exercise as you go along because you're now executing in the moment.

The titled attributes of this chapter are non-negotiable. You either have them, or you don't. If you find that you lack any of them, you'll have to figure out why that is. By this time you should know some of the questions to ask yourself. You may have even come across the answer while working on a different exercise. Either way now is the time to assess whether or not you are exercising the use of these attributes in as pure a form as possible, as it relates to you. The goal here is, to continue your work towards living life as your <u>best</u> you.

So let me ask you: (Try to be as detailed as possible when answering the questions)

- How confident are you in your ability to navigate this life as a whole?
- Do you have issues trusting others? If so, what is it that keeps you from trusting others?
- Do you find that there are times when you can't trust yourself? If so, what is it about yourself that you don't trust? If applicable, why do you believe this lack of trust exists?
- How often do you find yourself hoping for something?
- Do you hope from a place of faith or a place of doubt? Be honest with yourself. Try to be detailed about the "why" to your answer.
- What is your stance on faith? Start with what you believe faith to be and what it means to you.
- How often do you find yourself exercising faith? Does it come easily to you? Do you find it hard to do?
- Do you believe in yourself?
- Do you believe in this journey?
- Do you believe in your ability to complete this journey?
- How important is it to you and your quest, to implement the intentional use of these four attributes in your everyday life?

What is it to have trust, faith, and confidence in yourself? Belief right? (Aside from high self-esteem) How many of you have affirmed your belief in yourself while reading through this chapter? These are questions you should be answering in your notebook. Now how many of you were being openly honest with yourselves? How did your body respond to those thoughts? Did your heart skip a beat or did your heart rate increase? Did you feel a tingling sensation flow through you or in a particular part(s) of your body? Did you feel woozy at all?

I don't know how many of you actually pay attention to how your body responds to your thoughts, but I'm going to tell you, that if you've never paid attention to it before now, you should start. If you were already noticing how your body responds to your thoughts then good for you!

You ever pray to God wishing that he would respond to you . . . Immediately? So that you would know what to do in the moment? To be able to make a decision that you've been pondering for some time; or have that miracle manifested that you've been praying for?

It's to each his own, where this is concerned, in terms of who and how we worship and pray to. That's not the discussion here nor is it for judgment. We all have the right to our beliefs and understanding of life and will carry on with life accordingly. However, something I stand firm in is that we all have God within; and because of this fundamental fact, we can receive immediate responses to our "prayers."

Gut feelings, intuition, your "spidey" senses; these are all feelings that we get in response to something that causes us to take action in some form or manner. This feeling hits us from a belief. That's how our body responds to belief! Whether it be confirmation or warning, it's still a belief that caused your body to react.

When you genuinely believe something or believe in something, you will feel it. When you think about it, you will feel it. When you speak about it, you will feel it. Even when you dream about it, you will feel it! Stop and think about that. Seriously. A made up mind doesn't need any convincing. Feel the goosebumps?

When you have trust in someone or something, and you *believe* you do, you will *feel* it. When you have faith in something or someone, and you *believe* you do, you will *feel* it. When you have hope for something, and you *believe* in the possibilities of that hope, you will *feel* it. If you don't, then you should be checking your belief system. There's a disconnect somewhere.

Trust, faith, hope, and belief, like the blood in our veins and the heart that pumps that blood. Like the brain and sub-conscious that controls our bodily functions on auto, and like even, the very air that we breathe; trust, faith, hope, and belief are vital to living this life.

Epilogue

So. Here we are. We're now in the final chapter about to end; and you've made it to this point all because of that decision you made, the moment you decided to read this book. You've learned some things about me and hopefully, some things about yourself.

For me, it's the ending of a trip down memory lane. Thinking about the steps, routes and moment points that I've been through to make it to where I am right now. Organizing those thoughts, steps, paths and moment points so that I could share it with you. All in the hopes that it will be helpful to someone out there going through life's lessons; and to provide a nugget or two or three, that might be beneficial to any reader. I thank you for taking the time to read about my journey and for considering trying out some or all of the methods I used to help me grow. I hope that you were able to find something useful within the contents.

For you, no matter where you are in life, it's an opportunity to take stock of your moment points thus far. If your life has been what you deem to be a successful one then perhaps you've found a few points of view within the chapters that has given you something to think about. If your life has been one moment full of lessons after the other, then you now know that not only are you not alone but that it could always be worse. Additionally, you've just been presented with some options. Either way, I hope that everyone who reads the contents within this book, can pull something from it, that they're able to make use of in their lives.

We have a responsibility to ourselves, to make the best of our lives. Make use of the opportunities that present themselves to us. Increase and quench our innate thirst for knowledge. We also have a responsibility to society as human beings. We're all working at having and living a wonderful life, but we're also working for the greater good of the human race — the collective. When we work for the good of ourselves, we become better equipped and more beneficial to the whole. Likewise, when we work for the good of the whole, we inevitably benefit. As we too are a part of the whole.

In summation, anything I believe I can do, I can. It takes but a decision. In the case of not knowing how to do what I believe it is that I can do, I set out to learn how. From that point on I aim, always, to be the best that I can be at it. I aim to master it. I've always been one that likes to be positioned in such a way that no one can come and tell me about my 'stuff'. I have learned, however, while confidence in what I do is necessary, equally so, is the importance that I do not block myself from learning more — learning from those who may have some knowledge to offer; or those teachable moments where I can learn by observation or correction, from those who are more knowledgeable. Those who take the initiative to share alternatives or the proper way of doing something; and are also willing to show you *how*.

You may have come across a lot of statements you don't agree with while reading this book. To that I say, try to contemplate on it with an open mind. Let me also say this; the mind is capable of expanding much in the way that the universe expands. We gain more wisdom, knowledge, and understanding during our moment points. We can visualize on a broader scale and produce more ideas. We're stronger and more complex, yet we're ever learning and growing more. This expansion of our mind hasn't changed the physiology of our make-up.

So what is it that keeps a person from being able to adapt to change? Their inability to get past anything that goes against their constructed, conceptualized world and the knowing they have from within it. It's the classic fight of new information or thought, against personal beliefs and the perceived notion of knowing.

Things begin to get a little complex at this point because we are now dealing with the discussion of things not visible to our naked eyes. The kind of "things" not easily accepted by the psyche. Things that can only come to you by using your ability to "see" within. I understand the frustration. You start to feel like you're being spoken to in circles. You hear a bunch of words that seem to make no sense. I ask you to drop, not bear, but drop heart and have patience.

What I mean by that is, for me, I recognized that my emotions were at the root of my block. The reason why I was having such a hard time getting past understanding the words, my situations and moving on to my next moment points. You see, no one can tell you *how* to tap into your inner senses. I believe the experience is unique to the individual. Nor can anyone tell you how to adapt to change.

Yes, it can be worded and defined in such a way as to appear to give instruction, but in reading said instructions, you're not going to become armed with an ability immediately after reading it, automatically. For what it's worth, you probably wouldn't understand it, as understanding is also unique to the individual. Therefore, an explanation written down with the intent to give an instruction is based on the perception and understanding of the individual who's giving or writing it.

In a nutshell, this means that everything that I've written about, worked for me because it was intended for me. I learned along the way, and it resulted in what I've written about throughout this book. However, everything that I've written about, discovered and experienced was based on *my* perception and understanding of things. Knowing this can be frustrating, but that frustration can be surpassed. It's all up to you. It takes but a decision.

It can and will happen for some, quicker than it will for others. But try to remember that each journey is an individual one of which *you* set the pace. You will experience your moments when you are filled with understanding because you already have. It's just a matter of connecting the moments. Knowing this should help you to be patient while working towards manifesting it in the now because you now know, it's already done.

How do *I* know that you've gained understanding and will be successful while you're waiting for your moments to cross paths? Very simply because you are reading this! While I can't guarantee your *level* of success, I know that y*ou* made a decision that led to this very moment! Every single move we make is for a purpose and to an extent, by design — each step we take. Every move we make, puts into motion, the next sequence of events leading to the creation of the next set of our moment points.

You can take solace in the fact that you *will* gain understanding on a deeper level never experienced before. Just as soon as you let go and relinquish control. Trust the process. Drop it, release it and let it go. Giving in to yourself with an open mind is a process that cannot be willed. You will have to trust your inner senses to guide you on this journey. Trying to seek aid, assistance or instruction outside of yourself, will only delay the process. Not to disregard what I said before about seeking professional help if that's what you believe you need. I'm speaking more along the lines of asking your friends and family to help you connect with your inner self. It's a personal journey. Nothing and no-one can be the driving force behind *your* journey. Once again, your inner senses will guide you through this journey when you strive to connect with your inner self.

By the time you reach this point in the book, you should've already have started a chain of events that will serve to propel you towards the goals you set for yourself at the beginning of this journey. It's not an easy journey, but one that will be well worth the end result. Allow yourself the freedom to let your inner senses guide you while you work towards connecting with your inner self and the inherent power contained within. Remember, these are God-given gifts imparted to you at your creation. They are inherently yours! With just a bit of work, through the completion of the exercises presented to you throughout the book, you're on your way to living the life you've always wanted for yourself. So go on; what are you waiting for? You've made the decision. Now live in your greatness!

Bibliography

Angelou, Maya. Interview with Oprah Winfrey. The Oprah Winfrey Show, Oprah.com (2011) Video

Chopra, Deepak. "Daily Inspiration" Psychology Tomorrow Magazine. Stanley, Seigel, August 16, 2016. www.psychologytomorrowmagazine.com 2.20.2019

Dahl, Lynda Madden. Living A Safe Universe, Vol. 2. CA: The Woodbridge Group, 2013. Print

Henley, William Ernest. Book of Verses: Life and Death (Echoes). England: Book of Verses, 1888. Print

Nichols, Lisa and Jane Switzer. Abundance Now: Amplify Your Life and Achieve Prosperity. CA: Dey Street Books, 2015. Hardcover

Robbins, Mel. The 5 Second Rule: Transform Your Life, Work and Confidence with Everyday Courage. TX: Savio Republic, 2017. Print

Roberts, Jane. Seth Speaks: The Eternal Validity of the Soul. CA: Amber-Allen Publishing, 1972. Print

The Holy Bible, New Century Version. Copyright 1987, 1988, 1991 by Word Publishing, a Division of Thomas Nelson, Inc. Used by Permission

ABOUT THE AUTHOR

Mecheline Muhammad makes her debut as an author with her first published work, The Decision. She is also the owner and operator of a small natural bath and body business, which she has been operating since 2012. When she isn't making product or writing, which is a favorite past time of hers, she can be found reading about the ancients, studying the cosmos, working on a project that's somehow related to the universe or spending time with her family. She is currently working on her next book, Mastering Your Thoughts.

www.ingramcontent.com/pod-product-compliance
Lightning Source LLC
Chambersburg PA
CBHW071209070526
44584CB00019B/2971